Old Hopes
for a New Place

Old Hopes
for a New Place

THE LEGACY OF AREND D. LUBBERS
AT GRAND VALLEY STATE UNIVERSITY

Stephen Rowe, *Editor*

Michigan State University Press · *East Lansing*

♾ The paper used in this publication meets the minimum requirements of ANSI/NISO
Z39.48-1992 (R 1997) (Permanence of Paper).

 Michigan State University Press
East Lansing, Michigan 48823-5245

Printed and bound in the United States of America.

12 11 10 09 08 07 06   1 2 3 4 5 6 7 8 9 10

Catalofrom by the Library of Congress: LC Control Number 2005032538

Cover and book design by Sharp Des!gns, Inc., Lansing, MI

Front cover photograph is of Arend D. Lubbers, President of Grand Valley State University, January 1969 to June 2001. Photograph on the back cover is of the Cook Carillon
Tower with the Cook-DeWitt Center in the immediate background and looking toward
the Student Services Building and Henry and Padnos Halls on the Allendale campus,
Grand Valley State University.

g **green**
press
INITIATIVE Michigan State University Press is a member of the Green Press Initiative and is committed to developing and encouraging ecologically
responsible publishing practices. For more information about the Green Press Initiative
and the use of recycled paper in book publishing, please visit *www.greenpressinitiative.org*.

Visit Michigan State University Press on the World Wide Web at *www.msupress.msu.edu*

Contents

Foreword

L. William Seidman

I COMMEND TO YOU THE WISDOM OF AREND D. LUBBERS. HE SERVED AS a college president of exceptional insight, and as a public person of great virtue. He is also highly articulate. Reading his speeches is enjoyable and very effective for anyone who is concerned with education, public policy, and the moral/spiritual condition of our nation.

I first discovered President "Don" Lubbers when I traveled to Pella, Iowa, to meet the president of Central College. He was advertised to me as the youngest college president in the United States. This visit occurred because I was chairman of the board of what was then Grand Valley State College and had been asked by the board to lead the search for a new leader. Our first president, James Zumberge, had departed, and would later become president of USC. In my search, I had interviewed candidates from one end of the country to the other without much success; either they wanted a more established institution or we wanted a more exciting leader.

My first impression of Central College was good. In the flat lands of Iowa, the college had created a very attractive series of gardens leading into the campus. It turned out that President Lubbers's gardens were just a small sample of the many innovative and creative activities he had under-way at the college.

From our first meeting, I was convinced that Arend Lubbers was right for Grand Valley, and Grand Valley was right for him.

So it came to be; Don Lubbers came to Grand Valley to begin the creation of what is now a four-campus university with twenty thousand students and a reputation for excellence that has reached well beyond its home state.

As the sponsor of Lubbers for president, I watched with personal interest in how the new administrator was doing. Every time he gave a speech, I was elated with the college's choice. I was a bit of a connoisseur of college presidential speeches, since I had attended three universities— all big names—Harvard, Dartmouth, and the University of Michigan. I noted with some pleasure that Grand Valley's presidential pronouncements were clearer, more incisive, more innovative, and generally more interesting than those of the presidents of my alma maters.

As you read President Lubbers's statements in this book, I believe you will find them as thoughtful and interesting today as we found them when they were delivered.

Bringing Arend Lubbers to Grand Valley was the best thing that has happened to the university in its thirty-year history, and I am proud to have had a part in it.

It is my great privilege to have been associated with Don over the years. Reading these speeches will provide me and many others with the enjoyable experience of renewing our friendship and enforcing my statement that President Lubbers's speeches are worth reading and re-reading.

Acknowledgments

Thanks to friends and colleagues at Grand Valley State University for assistance in preparation of this book: Christopher Barbee, Robert Beasecker, Darla Bennett, Robert Schoofs, Bernadine Carey-Tucker, Jean Enright, Cheryl Jones, Teri Losey, and Daniel Royer.

Old Hopes
for a New Place

Education, Democratic Life, and Religion

Stephen Rowe

AREND D. LUBBERS WAS PRESIDENT OF AN UNUSUAL AND RAPIDLY developing state university for a long time—thirty-two years—and during a very significant period of American and global history—1969–2001. Vietnam, the Cold War, counterculture, energy crisis, financial crisis, Reaganism, Generation X, technological revolution. . . . Lubbers was there.

And Lubbers spoke. One significant element of his highly successful leadership style is that on a regular basis he articulated the goal of providing liberal education in a public context in relation to the currents of contemporary culture. His discourse was a modeling of the basic mission of the university, as stated in the catalogue: "Grand Valley State University seeks to achieve its undergraduate instructional mission through a liberal education curriculum that acquaints students with the tradition of humane values and the heritage, problems, and perspectives of their own and other cultures and that develops the lifelong skills of critical thinking, articulate expression, and independent learning." Lubbers practiced what he preached. He spoke as a person who is not only generally educated, but also liberally educated, a person who speaks as a citizen in the full sense of that term, to and with other citizens, as one who is cultivated in their humanity and committed to that same cultivation in others.

In this book we present a selection of the speeches of Arend "Don" Lubbers. The intended audience is not only the alumni and friends of Grand Valley State University. We offer this collection of speeches to the general public as well—a public that is still concerned with the life we share as citizens, rather than only their individual roles as private consumers and specialists. In this sense we present Lubbers in the American democratic tradition of the public intellectual, a tradition that is greatly at risk in an era structured by technology, cost-benefit assessment, and media-generated attention deficit.[1]

A university president is in a unique position to contribute to the understanding and revitalization of our public life. This is so because the university—or at least the university as Lubbers envisions it—is a microcosm of the larger world, seeking to embody the world in its ideal sense while preparing students for the world in its actual sense.[2]

Vision

William James said that "any author is easy, once you catch the center of their vision."[3] In the case of Lubbers, the author's vision is distinctly one of education and learning, supported by (and supportive of) a democratic understanding of public life, and grounded in a strong religious commitment. In Lubbers's speeches, these three interdependent components—education, democratic life, and religion—are present from the beginning. And yet in the unfolding of his career greater clarity and depth of articulation of each component is achieved successively. For this reason I will present the Lubbers vision in this order—with the understanding that the vision is one and undivided, a single entity with closely interdependent components.

EDUCATION

It is remarkable that Lubbers's orientation was very clearly and directly present from the very beginning—even when he first assumed the office of the presidency at the youthful age of thirty-seven. In his inaugural address of 1969, entitled "Some Old Hopes for a New Place," he said: "This college was built on a solid liberal arts basis and there it will stay. Liberal arts will be nourished as the central element of our tradition and protected from the service-oriented role that has diluted so many liberal arts programs around the nation," and "We are established as a teaching institution and that we will stay." Addressing the atmosphere that is necessary to the support of this mission, he spoke of "reasonable and tolerant human behavior" and "a spirit of reason and harmony," and said that "The success of this college, of all colleges, depends on the development of human relationships built on reason."

These are the themes of both speech and action that echoed consistently throughout Lubbers's career. Their full meaning and dimension became clear as "old hopes" came into dialogue with American culture and education in the three decades with which a millennium ended.

DEMOCRATIC LIFE

Assuming office in a time of great upheaval in society and culture,[4] Lubbers stated his position from the beginning: "colleges and universities are caught in the middle. The actions, study, and decisions that would move us toward new values in colleges, communities, and eventually perhaps in all of American society cannot take place in an atmosphere of threat." He also said that "we had better open our ears to student commentary," and that "this college will serve as nobody's foil."

Lubbers's understanding of the social-cultural circumstance of education in the 1970s was radical—ironically often more radical than that of many student protesters who threatened to turn universities into "battlefields." In the most general terms, Lubbers witnessed what he called a "historical drift," away from "value commitments" and into an orientation of negativism, depression, and "self before service." This was brought on by the fact that "man [*sic*] has been unable to form value and moral theories to encompass his new technological world," and by "the domination of his surroundings by materialism and expediency."

The chief and most dangerous manifestation of this condition is a "negative context in American society [that is] something much different from anything we have faced before." The difference lies in the vicious-circle quality of negativism: "Before any of our societal problems will be solved, we must first solve this problem of negativism." Lubbers sees this as a condition of the whole society, though one that is "overtly expressed by the young," as a refusal to accept the fact that "Man seems almost as willing to accept his own demise as a spiritual being in America as he was willing to watch nature fall to his technological conquest. His soul is becoming as polluted today as his environment." Part of this negative will-ing, or what Lubbers sometimes calls "moral malaise," is a "silence of philosophical and spiritual alternatives," and hence a sense in which protest is necessarily and unconsciously "assigned" to the young. Lubbers's firm but sympathetic understanding of students and student protest was evident from the beginning and throughout his career, as was his willing-ness to engage in dialogue with students rather than either capitulate or dismiss them.

Lubbers's prescription for this deeply troubled and new condition is democratic life, both public and personal. In his career he was a champion for the values of community and service, and the reclaiming of shared val-ues as the necessary core of civilized existence. His commitment to the unification of core values in democracy is very clear. For example, in his 1990 address at the fortieth anniversary of Sarajevo University, and on the occasion of his receiving an honorary degree, he said that "individual free-dom of thought and expression will be the 'bed rock' for any truly success-ful society in the future," and "How to govern democratically will be the question asked by people throughout the world. Democracy, government structured to reflect the will of the governed, will be on the minds of peo-ple now and in the twenty-first century. There will be few if any societies where the issue will not arise, and every autocrat and oligarchy will have to contend with the movement towards democracy." Faithful to this idea at home as well as abroad, Lubbers consistently emphasized community. In his 1972 commencement address he said that "The usual commence-ment address urges graduates to set their sights toward the stars. I ask you to look into yourselves and where you live and build community. . . . I urge you to find purpose and identity in helping people appreciate one another, by providing a psychological cement to hold good relationships together." Along with community, and as a fundamental way of overcoming the "moral malaise" of society, Lubbers also emphasized service, the necessity of moving beyond the "self before service" orientation of contemporary society.

Lubbers's understanding of democratic society is such that the humanities are necessary: "A democracy to survive in the future requires a high level of human understanding from its citizens." On several occasions he addressed this requirement in business contexts, as well as the recipro-cal relationship between the humanities and business/society. For example, at a 1983 Steelcase Corporation conference he said: "The humanities are necessary for business and society just as strong business in a stable soci-ety is the foundation for the pursuit of humanistic study."

The core values of democratic society, and the conviction that "a soci-ety cannot survive or at least be remembered as a society unless it has or leaves a record of its humanistic expression" are at the root of Lubbers's commitment to education: "Education is going to have to be an almost predominant aspect of the American way of life in the next twenty years. Americans must be able to understand the age in which they live, and guide it and control it for human purposes."

With this vital coincidence between democratic values and humanis-tic education, we come to the very heart of the Lubbers vision. Perhaps he stated it most fully in Sarajevo: "The twenty-first century is waiting for those open minds who know that there is no final revelation, but building on the best of what was believed and the experience of those who believed it will seek to gather more insight into the life of the spirit and the nature of the universe. They may find their understanding in an old structure that transforms itself or outside the formal structures established to tend the values and the mysteries. It will not matter. The success or failure of life in the twenty-first century, however, will depend on people finding values in common that will help them relate in spirit as they pursue their more tem-poral interests."

RELIGION

Lubbers's phrase, "life of the spirit," brings us to the third component of his vision: religion. And here, of course, we are not concerned with his private or personal religious orientation (an interesting story in itself, but a different one from the one we tell here), but rather his public or civil religion.[5]

According to Lubbers, "learning moves in two directions: first, it leads to objective, new knowledge for all who care to contemplate it; second, it adds to an individual's capacity for deeper personal understanding." The second direction Lubbers identifies as a deepening of spirit: "It makes one more sensitive and brings with it a fullness of spirit." At other points Lubbers relates this crucial second direction to Socratic wisdom, which he defines as "the ability to discover inner qualities and relationships."

"Fullness of spirit" is associated with a basic distinction between knowledge and understanding. Knowledge is that which is settled and generally accepted, the findings of science and the canons of literature, that which is relatively stable and given. Understanding is more personal, and occurs through knowledge but beyond that which can be certified as a function of memory, or repetition, or mind alone. Understanding entails openness to new discovery and transformation of the whole person: "Understanding properly sought, learned, and applied contributes to the transformation of people and, thus, to their spiritual growth."

Because of this essential religious aspect of education and its intimate relationship with democracy, Lubbers identifies the work of the university as a "sacred profession": "Ours is a sacred profession because we are involved in a force that shapes the future for individuals and society—the aspirations of our students." Here we come to the fullness of Lubbers's vision, and the sense in which everything he says about education is embraced within a single statement: "There is no more important profession than the one that deals with knowledge in the search for truth and understanding."

Legacy

The university developed by Arend Lubbers is grounded in the liberal arts, in a commitment to teaching, and in general education for all students conducted in the mode of liberal education—which is applied beyond traditional liberal arts subjects to all domains of knowledge, including professional. Most essentially, for Lubbers, the "deepening of spirit" at the center of his vision and vocation involves relationship—as evidenced, for example, when he explicates the deepening as "understanding of relationships between and among people, and for a relationship to nature." Anyone who has worked with Don is impressed and amazed by the range and substance of his relationships, and the sense in which they exhibit that most persuasive American quality of presence that Martin Marty—following Justice Felix Frankfurter—identifies as "cohesive sentiment."[6]

Given his essential relationality, it seems appropriate to conclude this introduction to Arend Lubbers's speeches with response, specifically response in terms of the continuation of his legacy in the present and future.

Glenn Niemeyer, who served with Lubbers as vice president and provost for almost his entire administration (1973–2001), remarked late in his own career that many programs in the university, especially those oriented to the professions, specialized training, and career preparation, would do just fine on their own. The liberal arts, however, if they are to thrive in the environment of the contemporary university and society, require protection and support. The Lubbers legacy can be appreciated in this light as an ongoing protection and support—at the very least as a strong reminder of grounding and source. This legacy is an integral part of a history and a tradition that any but the most short-sighted or opportunistic would wish to honor in the present and future. Lubbers speaks both from and to the center of our integrity and identity, our success and our service.

But what does it mean, in practical terms, for us to honor and remain faithful to our core identity in a swirling world of assessment, market analysis, and temptation to regard students as more or less happy consumers—not to mention a very generalized atmosphere of specialization that Alfred North Whitehead has described in terms of a new "celibacy of the intellect"?[7] I would like to conclude this essay by offering two humble suggestions.

First, we need clarity about our basic commitments. John Dewey, speaking from the middle of the last century, said that the chief problem of the public in large-scale developed societies is intellectual.[8] What he meant by this is that to some considerable degree, our problem is one of vision—of articulating in ways that are actionable purposes associated with cultivation of the person, community, and humane values, in the midst of a society and universities that are dominated by technology, specialization, and commercialism.

At GVSU in the present there are very promising signs that something like this is occurring. Our new provost, Gayle Davis, has begun her administration with strategic planning. The very term is frightening to some, insofar as it connotes quantification, market analysis, and the temptation to begin everything anew—the specter of reorganization. This, however, is not what she means. The provost's efforts are simply to gather together the various mission statements, fragments of oral tradition, etc., and bring to articulation the basic purposes and commitments of the university. This is precisely the intellectual job that Dewey recommends— and what a provost and leader of academic and learning community might be expected most fundamentally to do.

Another promising sign, with respect to articulating our fundamental reason for being, is that our new president, Mark Murray, has begun to assume a leadership position in a learning community at the heart of the university. His speaking has not been detached or general, but rather in the context of specific issues and events in the life of the university. For example, in his remarks to an evening candlelight vigil on the anniversary of 9/11 he said: "I ask you to reflect on the redemption that occurred in the time after September 11. It was a better way to live. Reflection on basic truths. Commitment to making our communities better. Reaching out to others. Looking at yourself in some fear and anxiety, and asking what mattered most to you. Looking beyond yourself to basic and yet transcendent values of freedom, courage, integrity, understanding, compassion. Being prepared to make sacrifices for these higher values. You are here at Grand Valley to make a better life for yourself and others. There were lessons in those days about what a better life is. Reflect on them." Here the university speaks, not about itself but *as itself*. Here basic commitments are alive and active, enacted, embodied—not just admired as abstract objects on a shelf in the inner sanctum.

My second suggestion is that we stay focused on direct service to students, our actual relationships in classrooms and advising and the pulsing life of learning community. There are many temptations to stray from our service, some associated with students themselves and the tendency I mentioned—to be overly concerned with their "happiness" or consumer satisfaction.

Hannah Arendt, thinking about the worldwide crisis of authority that came to light in the twentieth century and the qualities that are necessary to a healthy polity, distinguishes between "force" and "power."[9] Force, involving coercion, violence, and the threat thereof, comes from the top down. It imposes. Power is more gentle, more subtle, persuasive—and ultimately stronger. My point is that our success at GVSU has not been the result of big donations, elegant buildings, efficient administration, ambitious committees, or favorable conditions in the legislature—though these things can be very helpful. Rather, our success and our power have arisen out of our relationships with students—one by one, class by class, event by event.

These two suggestions and reports of work in progress indicate the continuing vitality of the Lubbers's legacy and the strength of its momentum. In this regard it is important to take note of the amazing continuity of his vision throughout his tenure as president. His last official speech to the campus community in April of 2001 invokes the very same sense of mission that he articulated in the 1969 inaugural address: "When I arrived here thirty-two years ago last January, I found a faculty devoted to the liberal arts and a college with a core curriculum that reflected that devotion. As I leave, the university, now complex, now home for professional programs defined by their excellence, I leave with the liberal arts core changed, but excellent and intact."

How could he do this?—maintain such consistency and perseverance in the face of endless distractions and conflicting imperatives: emphasize graduate programs, professional programs, fundraising at any cost, research—the list goes on. I conclude this introduction to his speeches with the suggestion that the answer to this question lies in his religious values. Again, here I do not speak of religious values in the private and personal sense, though these are certainly fundamental to Lubbers the person and his being in the world. The religious values to which I refer are those more general, public, and ecumenical values that can be affirmed and celebrated by those of any faith tradition—and indeed by anyone who maintains a belief in the dignity and possibility of the human spirit.

In August of 1982 Don gave a very clear summary of three root religious values. The first is "Keep the Faith," by which he means "a belief that man's seeking will lead to useful discovery, that what we do not know may be known for the enrichment of man. . . . Man must believe in himself and the worthiness of the life given him."

The second value is "Think Rationally": "One does not have to believe that rational conscious thought is the only means to understanding or knowing. . . . [but] most trouble in the world emanates from man's failure to use the power of his reason. . . . The bad consequences of good discoveries and insight can usually be traced to the breakdown of reason, and the rampage of emotion unchecked."

Lubbers's third root religious value is "Respect Mystery": "Reason may unravel mystery, but there is always more that is unknown and mysterious to be unraveled. What we don't know, yet anticipate, holds us in awe. At least it should. Those who do not respect mystery usually lack humility." Respecting mystery also makes it possible for us to "be aware of and respect strong and deep feelings that we cannot yet understand," and "it is also to bask in the wonder, love, and joy of life without understanding it all."

Tu Weiming, one of the great world citizens of our era, speaks of a new enlightenment period of humankind that is emerging not through the imposition of abstract universals on all peoples, but rather through what he calls "the globalization of local knowledge."[10] The Lubbers legacy is a very good example of Professor Tu's point, including his suggestion that we need "thick" dialogue with the full particularity of place and time—rather than the thinness of mere intellectual exchange and easy generalizations. With Lubbers and the case of Grand Valley State University, we have wisdom and guidance from the thickness of the actual adventure of building and maintaining an educational institution for all peoples, one in which their whole humanity is cultivated—certainly including their professional life, but their broader humanity as well.

The Lubbers legacy will continue to inspire and guide us at GVSU. But it could also be helpful to others, perhaps more so than books or seminars on "how to be a successful college president," or "how to make your public institution distinguished." Lubbers's work demonstrates and radiates the dignity of the local, and what the Greeks called *phronesis*, that highest form of wisdom which is only manifest in the particulars of actual life. It also demonstrates how the universal qulity of Lubbers' "old hopes" can become available through the local, and powerfully available— more deeply than only ideas to be "applied," but as that vital alignment of vision and vitality we know as hope.

NOTES

1. On the role of the public intellectual in American history, see William Dean, *The Religious Critic in American Culture* (Albany, N.Y.: SUNY Press, 1994).

2. For perspective on both ideal and actual relationships between university and society in America, and the role of the president therein, see A. Bartlett Giamatti, *A Free and Ordered Space: The Real World of the University* (New York: Norton, 1988).

3. William James, *Essays on Radical Empiricism and a Pluralistic Universe* (New York: Dutton, 1971), 163.

4. For an interpretation of this crucial period in American history, see my *Leaving and Returning: On America's Contribution to a World Ethic* (Lewisburg, Pa.: Bucknell University Press, 1989).

5. On American civil religion, see Elwyn A. Smith, ed., *The Religion of the Republic* (Philadelphia: Fortress Press, 1971) and Martin E. Marty, *Righteous Empire* (New York: Doubleday, 1970). More specifically, in terms of the variant of civil religion that Lubbers represents, see William Dean, *The Religious Critic in American Culture* (Albany: SUNY Press, 1994); John K. Roth, *Private Needs, Public Selves: Talk About Religion in America* (Chicago: University of Illinois Press, 1997); and Reinhold Niebuhr, *The Children of Light and the Children of Darkness* (New York: Charles Scribner's Sons, 1970).

6. Martin E. Marty, *The One and the Many: America's Struggle for the Common Good* (Cambridge, Mass.: Harvard University Press, 1997), 19, 22, 212–25.

7. Alfred North Whitehead, *Science and the Modern World* (New York: Free Press, 1967), 197.

8. John Dewey, *The Public and Its Problems* (Chicago: Swallow Press, 1927), 126.

9. Hannah Arendt, *On Violence* (New York: Harcourt, Brace and World, 1970), 35–56.

10. Tu Weiming, "Implications of the Rise of 'Confucian' East Asia," in *Daedalus* 129, no. 1 (Winter 2000): 195–218. See also his commentary in Peimin Ni and Stephen Rowe, *Wandering: Brush and Pen in Philosophical Reflection* (Chicago: Dong Fang and Art Media Resources, 2002).

Some Old Hopes for a New Place

OCTOBER 12, 1969

I T IS DIFFICULT TO GIVE A NEW COLLEGE IDENTITY. THIS PROBLEM IS especially perplexing because a good educational institution should have an individuality it shares with no one else. The identity of a college is largely a question of feelings. It is perhaps the nostalgic feeling that an alumnus has when he thinks back on his college years. Identity is what is in the minds of scholars as they decide the college to which they want to dedicate the productive years of their learning, research, and teaching. A college's identity is on a youngster's mind as he decides the academic environment in which he will spend four years of his life. Parents consider identity as they help determine one of the most crucial parts of their child's life: his education. A college's identity can be bad as well as good, a liability as well as an asset. And because of its importance, it is something that deserves sustained attention. A college's identity is the mark of distinction that will carry it to success and respect, or will degrade and stultify it.

What shall we concern ourselves with as we build an identity for Grand Valley State College? A part of a college's individuality is its physical plant: its buildings—the way in which the bricks and mortar are put together. Here we are very fortunate. The buildings that we are dedicating today are two of many splendid structures on this campus. We are very proud of our campus facilities, and their unique architecture. Our pride is evident in the way that these facilities are being preserved, and will continue to be preserved. The buildings on this tract give something with which a person can identify; they are not the hard and sterile surroundings that so many newly built colleges face.

Another part of a college's identity is its location. Again, we are fortunate for the foresight of this college's founders. We have room to grow. That is a statement few colleges can make today. In addition, nature has given us some very pleasant surroundings. There is something, I think, to the age-old idea that a bit of splendid isolation catalyzes the intellectual spirit.

Another factor in our identity is the area in which our college rests. Once more we can consider ourselves fortunate. We have a thriving urban center near our college. We are near the Great Lakes that provide some of the best vacation spots in the world. From this area we have found businesses, industries, unions, and foundations that have lent substantial support to the establishing of the college, and to its preservation. Few colleges can claim the dedicated community support that Grand Valley has been given.

So far, however, I have left out a vital element in a college's identity, the element that is perhaps most important of all: people—people and their interrelationships. No matter how computerized and technical the world becomes, the interrelationships between people are still the primary factors that determine success and failure, peace and war, love and hate. It is this human environment at Grand Valley State College that I want to discuss at some length.

A president is supposed to provide leadership for a college. What is leadership? It is initiating programs; it is recommending curriculum; it is assigning budget priorities; it is guiding the appointment of staff; it is deciding building sites. But to me, before any of these things, leadership is something even more important: it is the motivation of a spirit of reason and harmony in the academic milieu. For this spirit puts a whole new light on budget, staff, and building negotiations.

As we address ourselves to establishing at Grand Valley an atmosphere of reasonable and tolerant human behavior, we face a trying task. Despair has grown in the midst of the affluence that characterizes this nation. The tremendous optimism upon which this country was founded and which propelled its westward movement, its industrialization, and its triumph in two world wars is dimming. It has become starkly evident in the 1960s that, while technology has brought us bridges and new hospitals, it has also brought us the H-bomb and Napalm. It is not only the weapons of war that have emerged to chill the mechanical optimism of the twentieth century. Modern life has proven to be harried, disruptive, and inductive to nervous tension. At the heights of our mechanical success, we saw our astronauts exhibit before our eyes the boundless freedom and fearlessness of man. But even as we watched the television, we sat locked in our own homes, afraid to walk the city streets, even in our own neighborhoods.

Our educational institutions were for generations the focal point of the nation's social and industrial optimism. They turned out the trained minds that built our complicated modern society. But they have not escaped from the spreading despair. They are, in fact, in the middle of the descent in the maelstrom. The conflict inherent in the outside society has incited simultaneously a vicious indictment of the entire American educational system. The same reason that young people see for despair in the world outside the university they see writ just as large inside. They rebel at standardized mass production courses. They rebel at bureaucratic multiversities that depersonalize academic material. They rebel at degrees becoming yardsticks of personal worth. They rebel at the endless lists of reciped articles and books which repeat again that which has already been repeated many times, or that which should not have been written at all. They rebel, in fact, at the whole idea that education provides solutions to society's problems.

The old social and educational order is being attacked by some and is being in turn defended by others, and the forces meet on the college campus. Institutions of higher learning have become battlefields, and the war is not always one of clashing intellects. The critics of the old order have not been content with scholarly formulations. Action, often violent, has instead taken the place of the educational process. Those who protect the old order find themselves equally drawn into the emotional context, and violence on one side has often bred violence on the other.

Sometimes I feel that the forces that surround us verge on being out of control. We live in an atmosphere ridden on one hand with senseless and unthinking condemnations of today's youth movements. On the other hand, we find youthful demonstrators talking of revolution without ever having seen a copy of Marx or Lenin, fighting mindlessly against an undefined "establishment." I am reminded intellectually of being on Matthew Arnold's Dover Beach where:

> . . . we are here as on a darkling plain
> Swept with confused alarms of struggle and flight
> Where ignorant armies clash by night.

It is time we gathered our wits, for the polemics sound too harsh and the hand is becoming too quick on all sides to follow the bitterness of the words. Students occupy buildings, legislatures take away funding, and the colleges and universities are caught in the middle. The actions, study, and decisions that would move us toward new values in colleges, communities, and eventually perhaps in all of American society cannot take place in an atmosphere of threat. We must free ourselves of the emotional actions and reactions that are beginning to characterize this nation's social life and politics. I do not mean to imply that conflict can be totally eliminated. History clearly shows that conflict is inevitable in human life. The problems are how conflict is resolved and the environment in which it takes place.

Inaugural addresses are often pep rallies in which a side is endorsed and the enemy invoked. My message today is just the reverse. I am not here to take sides. I see the office of president of a college as a place where the inevitable human conflicts are arbitrated and issues settled. Let me bring some issues to beat to illustrate what I mean. I have been told by some that this college must choose between liberal arts and specialized or technical training. How many colleges have been fooled or pushed into a bifurcation of this issue? Is this college to take up the sword for liberal arts while ignoring a society that demands from its schools the trained personnel to keep our economy alive? Or are we to man the barricades for technical training at the expense of educating the critical and historically conscious minds that a healthy democracy demands? I will endorse neither such approach. This college was built on a solid liberal arts basis and there it will stay. Liberal arts will be nourished as the central element of our tradition and protected from the service-oriented role that has diluted so many liberal arts programs all around the nation. But the area that surrounds us, and the nation, demand technical and specialized training from their educational institutions, and we are moving to provide this training too. We are proud of our Urban Affairs Institute, our Business Internship Program, and our Teacher Education Center. We are anticipating several more institutes and centers which will provide our college with a close link to the urban and industrial milieu that surrounds us.

What about the omnipresent issue of student protest? Shall we grant every student demand, or shall we call in the troops to quiet any student who questions authority? Either action is an opportunistic attempt to keep students' mouths shut about what is wrong in the university and the world. I think we had better open our ears to student commentary on our college policies. After all, no one can accuse the American college in this generation of being so successful that it does not need some criticism. I further believe we should ensure a student voice in the college decisions. I am going to encourage, as best I can, close contact with the students by both faculty and administration. We are adding students regularly to college committees. Students helped us draw up the rules and regulations handbook, and now that it is made they will have the opportunity of helping us decide where changes will have to be made in its content. We're listening, and we're changing, but that doesn't entail being pushed around by ideologues whose aim is not improvement and understanding, but the destruction of educational institutions. I stand behind every student who believes that a college should not act as a mouthpiece for the current regime and its values. The university has an intellectual commitment to truth and objectivity to uphold, grounded in centuries of scholarly toil. But I also say to that same student, neither should the university, through threat and coercion, become the unwitting ally of an ideology of anti-government and anti-establishment views. This college will serve as nobody's foil.

Yet another crisis subject. Are we to take up the research battlecry, hoping for institutional fame, while we skip over the academic dead bodies of dismissed professors who could not complete a book in time? Or shall we defend some vague concept of "good teaching" against research and publication, with the results of a lackluster academic environment in which critical minds dim as class notes grow yellowed with passing years? Neither of these routes makes academic sense. We are established as a teaching institution and that we will stay. We are working to guarantee that excellent teaching will be rewarded in promotion and tenure considerations. But we will also encourage responsible scholarship and research, knowing that conducted within the bounds of reason, and without the presence of threat, it will stimulate better classroom teaching.

How about the old issue of the relationship between the college and the state in which it resides? Are we wards of the legislature, the state, and the community, ready to bow to their every wish humbly? Or are we an intellectual fortress removed from the surrounding areas, and ready to fight off public pressures if necessary? My answer is that a college is a unique place, for it is a center of learning and critical examination of all that surrounds it. It is a place in the midst of our bustling society where ideas are allowed to flow freely without regard of consequence, and where increased understanding of a subject or problem is advanced as the highest value of our pursuits. And I will stake my job on the protection of this freedom. But to act as if we are an island is absurd.

We are not immune from the community and state in which we reside, or from state and local laws. Neither are we immune, and here is something so many colleges conveniently forget in fits of educational chauvinism, from the opportunities available in our community and in our state. We will ask to be recognized as a unique learning institution. But we will attempt, on the other hand, to show our goodwill toward the community, the state, and its agents. They, after all, nourish us; they give us the opportunity to learn and study. And to the easily forgotten taxpayer who gets a little less money to take home each month so that we may have the opportunity to dedicate these new buildings today, I feel no loss of pride in saying, "Thank you, we need you, and we appreciate your help."

The success of this college, of all colleges, depends on the development of human relationships built on reason. The environment must be open and honest, and the ethos conducive to the free flow of ideas. There must be respect for individuals, no matter how much you deplore their points of view. We want an atmosphere where a mistake in your work doesn't cost your job, but instead elicits help from colleagues to accomplish your tasks. Students should be considered the young scholars and thinkers that they are, not regarded as second class citizens to be punished for failure to imitate the values and mores of professors and administrators. I want an environment where as president of the college, I can openly express my opinions to faculty members and other administrators, for they will understand that I do not expect my views to be theirs. I believe we can build an environment free from coercion, free from battle cries, and free from the vicious actions and reactions that have characterized too many college campuses in recent years. This environment would give us an identity worthy of any college. A college community with this environment not only would have a better chance of academic distinction, but would earn the respect and appreciation of the state it serves.

Working toward such an identity will be hard in this crisis-ridden society, and we don't even expect our success to be immediate or complete. But I am a strong believer in what is sometimes called the "long haul," and we will be tenacious. Saying that reason can prevail in human affairs and become the watchword in an institutional system is a statement of hope. And in spite of our educational and social problems, I don't mind making it exactly that. Where will this nation and its educational system be until hope returns to human affairs, and a note of optimism once more enters the dialogue of our young people? As I speak of this, I remember a verse from Carl Sandburg:

> *This old anvil—the people, yes.*
> *This old anvil laughs at many broken hammers.*
> *There are men who can't be bought.*
> *There are women beyond purchase.*
> *The fireborn are at home in fire.*
> *The stars make no noise.*
> *You can't hinder the wind from blowing.*
> *Time is a great teacher.*
> *Who can live without hope?*

The Modern Day
Morality Play

ALLEN PARK COUNCIL OF CHURCHES

ALLEN PARK, MICHIGAN

MARCH 1970

I GUESS THAT IF I WERE TO SUCCINCTLY STATE MY MESSAGE TODAY, IT would be: "deliver us from further progress." This phrase is a conscious imitation of the title of a little-known philosophical work by Swedish writer Karl Tjerlov-Knudsen. Professor Tjerlov-Knudsen claimed that the Western world is drifting away from moral and spiritual commitments, and that this drift is having dilatory effects upon the future of Western man. I was fascinated to find in the book's introduction the brutally frank comment that "I am writing because I must say something, but I know that the world will little note my words." I turned back to the cover of the book, and found that it had been written in 1962. At the time when I removed it from the busy library where it was housed, it was 1967, and I was the first person to have used the book.

I want to start today from the theme in this remarkably perceptive little tract, for I think we are drifting away from value commitments in American society, and as Professor Tjerlov-Knudsen indicated and the obscurity of his book verified, there seem to be very few people who are seriously concerned about this trend in history. Americans have made the mistake of assigning truth to the ability of the intellect to manipulate material surrounds, and put them to practical use. Man's fascination with the power over nature yielded to him by his scientific achievements has led to scientific advances in recent generations that have become so rapid that we are almost entirely awed by their proportions. The eventual result of these tremendous scientific advances, and the accompanying technological progress, was very simply that man has found himself today incapable of understanding the world that surrounds him. The gadgetry and machinery that comprise the environment in which we live become obsolescent, and are replaced far more quickly than we can react and adapt to the new circumstances. Because man has been unable to form value and moral theories to encompass his new technological world, he has been unable not only to understand his situation, but more importantly than that, he has been unable to control or guide it. Our society today is what only can be called a historical drift.

As we face an age in which we have lost control of our environment, it would almost seem that man would rise up in anger against the domination of his surroundings by materialism and expediency. Yet in the face of the technological age in which we live, there has been a queer silence of philosophical and spiritual alternatives. Man seems almost as willing to accept his own demise as a spiritual being in America as he was willing to watch nature fall to his technological conquest. His soul is becoming as polluted today as his environment.

It's not that the Christian values that form the basis of the American way of life have been entirely forgotten; we still have people who are concerned enough to talk about the direction of American life. But where is the real concern with spiritual and cultural questions in a nation that is almost fanatically preoccupied with material activities? The famous philosopher Alfred North Whitehead has written: "All thought concerned with social organization expresses itself in terms of material things and of capital. Ultimate values are excluded. They are politely bowed to and then handed over to the clergy to be kept for Sundays."

Our love for material things is becoming a kind of idolatry, in the true biblical sense of the word. Philosopher Gabriel Marcel writes: "I ought to emphasize that there is no point in thinking of technical progress as being in itself an expression of sin. On the other hand, it is clear that technical progress is increasingly tempting man to claim for his achievements an intrinsic value that cannot really belong to them. Quite simply, we can say that there is great danger of technical progress making men into idolaters." The American society is increasingly held together by a nationwide concern with social economic status and making a living. It is decreasingly held together by a common commitment to the values, beliefs, and goals of our Judeo-Christian heritage. It has been the phenomenon of the late 1960s that it has been our youth who have finally decried the moral and ethical vacuum in our society. We in the meantime have been watching too much the long hair and beards, and listening too closely to the barbarous language. We have not thought carefully enough of what lies behind these tortured young men and women. I find it personally very disconcerting to preach to youngsters about moral decay when I, and my generation, are under indictment for the same charge. If you would doubt that there is some validity behind our youngsters' contempt for society, let me drag out a little of America's dirty linen in the form of popular slogans and idioms.

We instill our children with ideas of equality. The good old American slogan is "every man's as good as the next," and yet we know that those who do not achieve "the American success story" have a difficult time being as good as the next man. Those who do not go "from rags to riches" are often despised as having something wrong with them. While he is told about democracy in Government class, a student soon finds that it is a very bad idea to question the way the principal runs the school. And so we get the converse versions of the "this is a democratic county" slogan as shown in the equally good old American slogans, "keep your eyes open, and your mouth shut," or "you'll get more flies with honey than you will with vinegar."

We tell our children that this is a country with "free speech," where a person is able to say without fear how he feels about political, social, and moral matters. And so the first time that one of our youngsters explains his opposition to the war in Vietnam, he is accused of "not supporting the boys on the fighting front," or "aiding and abetting the communist cause." We tell our youngsters that they, the people, are the nation's rulers. At the same time, when they question foreign policy matters, they are told that "they do not know as much as our leaders," and "to follow the advice of the experts." We tell our youngsters that in order to be good citizens they must be informed citizens, and then they are told that information is "being withheld in the national interest." Americans praise themselves for "giving the other guy a fair shake," and "being honest," but youngsters rapidly find out that organized crime syndicates make more than large car companies. They discover that if you don't play the economic game, you are suddenly subject to the other side of America's double standard phraseology, and are admonished that "he's too honest" or "a fool and his money are soon parted." Americans extol the virtues of "the plain folks." Yet our youngsters soon realize that they are supposed to show respect and admiration for the guy who "made a success of himself."

When I think about this double standard in the American way of life, the great gap between what we preach and what we practice as adults, I have great empathy with the youth rebellion. But today we see an even more pitiful commentary on our times: our younger generation's protest, so well founded in the basis of its criticism, has itself degenerated into a wandering, aimless, goal-less system of social behavior. The protest has yielded no plans for the future. The answer to the materialist and bureaucrat is certainly not the freaked-out drug user. The answer to a militaristic foreign policy is certainly not broken windows, bombed out police stations, and vile language. The protest that we needed against an increasingly valueless society has itself become valueless. And so as we approach the 1970s, we are in a historical impasse. We live in a vacuum of social, political, and religious belief. America is becoming a nation with a very confused identity. So where do we go now in our polarized nation? Surely we do not want to remain on opposite sides of the fence from the young, nor do I think they really want to continue the generation gap any more than we do. It seems to me that both the old and the young are under indictment for the same charge: the failure to carry out action which is commensurate with their goals, values, and ideals. Perhaps if we admit that we have a common problem, the young and old can find a common solution. But this solution is going to take human energy, human time, human resources, and human money. First, the sooner we realize that there are no technical solutions to human problems, the better off we will all be as human beings, and the closer will be our ties with our growing youngsters.

The money we are pouring into the ghettos can't in itself eliminate human misery and poverty. How surprised we have been in the last generation when we built splendid new housing developments in the ghetto, only to see these in turn become ghettos in the next five years. Without a change in the attitudes and feelings, and willingness to contribute by people who are in positions to do so all across America, we are not going to solve any of our problems of equality.

We are not devoid of progress. There are those of us, mostly our youngsters, who are sacrificing their own material well-being to help those less fortunate by birth and education. I know of young men and women living and teaching in the ghetto so that they might, even in some small insignificant way, begin to span the gap between the rich and the poor, the educated and the uneducated. But we are not doing enough, and the examples of which I cite are far too few.

Secondly, in our corporate and organizational life, we must begin to demand the democratic and humanitarian goals that we endorse as constitutional prerogatives in the nation. The fact that a man works for a large corporation should make him no more subject to the tyranny of that corporation than it should to the larger organization of the federal government. As William White put it in his now famous book, *The Organizational Man*, it is not organization itself that is that cause of frustration and alienation; the problem is the unwillingness of the people who are within the organization to preserve their dignity, their respectability, and their courage in the face of what sometimes seem to be overwhelming and anonymous forces. I have a friend who recently sent me a copy of a plan being followed in the corporation of which he is president. In this firm, the most democratic processes are encouraged in everything from profit allocation to innovative techniques. He reports astounding success. Initiative and individuality are increasing, as are the profits of his business. And yet this example is far too rare on the American scene.

Thirdly, we need a revitalized interest in our communities. It is the community that has always been the core of American's democratic strength. Over a hundred years ago, Alexis de Tocqueville, the famous French philosopher, visited America and wrote *Democracy in America*. In this book, de Tocqueville states that the strength of the growing and thriving America was the initiative of the many communities of which it was comprised. We need interest in the community for integrating our schools, for solving our problems of pollution, for making playgrounds and recreation centers.

Fourth, and finally, and I believe most importantly, we need education. Education is going to have to be an almost predominant aspect of the American way of life in the next twenty years. Americans must be able to understand the age in which they live, and guide it and control it for human purposes. This comprehension can only come through learning, learning from the first years of a youngster's life, until the day when he passes from our society. One of our most trying problems in current America is not even so much the education of the young; it is the re-education of the middle aged and the elderly. Education is the key to giving the poor jobs; education is the key to a broader prospective on race relations; education is the key to being able to comprehend and thrive in a corporate organization; education is the key to being a demanding and intelligent citizen in voting and participating on public questions; education is the key to seeing, understanding, and following the problems of foreign affairs. Ralph Barton Perry, a well-known literary critic, has written of education and society: "the extent to which a man is free depends in the first place upon the extent to which he is aware of the possibilities. We must enlarge the span of man's consciousness by acquainting him both with the world and with the best that has been known and thought in the world. The free man must enjoy possession of his natural, intellectual, and moral inheritance."

Negativism as a Factor
in United States History

UAW, REGION I-D SUMMER SCHOOL AT BLACK LAKE

ONAWAY, MICHIGAN

AUGUST 12, 1970

I WANT TO SHARE WITH YOU TODAY SOMETHING THAT HAS FOR ME become an overwhelming concern. I am convinced at this point that a single historical factor is increasingly shaping the context of our lives in the United States. This factor is what I call "negativism."

As a college president, I spend many of my days in conferences with a variety of different people talking about many different subjects. As the last few years have gone by, more and more the dominant part of these conversations seems to focus on the subject of what's *wrong* with society, politics, and people in general. The constant topic of conversation is what the kids call "hang-ups." Sometimes the hang-ups are on very personal matters, such as how the society has repressed natural sexual outlets, and sometimes the hang-ups are very general ones shared by millions of people, like the war in Vietnam. These hang-ups are very dominant factors in how a person, or how a group of persons, will act under certain circumstances. Today, action-dominating and forcing hang-ups have come to seriously threaten positive voices and activities, and they have led to dissent, protest, and alienation.

I contend that this negative context in American society is something much different from anything we have faced before. In the past, America has always been characterized by its great optimism. Philosopher Robert Heilbroner, in his well-known book, *The Future as History*, was one of the first to historically document this fact. Even in the 1930s the underlying hope and expectation that things would get better helped the United States entrench and survive a Great Depression and the emergence of a tremendous world war. I guess I might get my point across best by asking a rhetorical question: What would have happened to the United States during the Depression if the attitudes that prevailed then were the ones that prevail now? I suspect our nation's survival could have been seriously threatened.

As I speak, the era of *student* protest and *student* dissent naturally comes to everyone's mind. But even though I am going to concentrate on the more conspicuous and easier to define youth involvement in nega-tivism, I want to make clear that I am talking about a national phenome-non. As a matter of fact, in order to prevent any of us from too easily settling back and blaming everything on the youngsters, which by the way is another form of negativism prevalent in our society, I am going to hypothesize that the kids have inherited much of their bitterness from their elders. A sociologist's look at America in the last generation illus-trates the source of negativism in our youth.

Youngsters today enter a pent-up and frustrated life that is far from being psychologically healthy. Young people find a society tantalized by gimmicks and entertainment that only the moneyed can enjoy. They find huge metropolitan areas and spend their few vacation days a year franti-cally escaping from the city in order to catch a glimpse of a mountain or river. They see factory assembly lines where workers become separated from the product they are making and as a result often feel alienated from their work. They find a society so mobile that few people have any place they can call home. They see our teeming ghettos where even survival is difficult. Our young see a nation with a fantastic abundance of natural resources that has squandered too much of its natural wealth in a period of a few generations. They see a nation that has always been the world spokesman for peace, fighting a war in Indochina for reasons that can only be vaguely explained. Children find that human love has an attempted

replacement in material bribes. Young folks look at fathers who are societal successes and consider them failures, because even if the father has
attained personal wealth, he has not acquired self-satisfaction, fulfillment,
or happiness. Saul Bellow, one of America's best novelists, frequently
documents this source of negativism in the society. Let me quote from
Bellow's *Seize the Day* as he portrays the feelings of a metropolitan busi-
nessman at a meeting:

> Uch! How they love money, thought Wilhelm. They adore money! Holy
> money! Beautiful money! It was getting so that people were feeble-
> minded about everything except money. While if you didn't have it you
> were a dummy, a dummy! You had to excuse yourself from the face of the
> Earth. Chicken! That's what it was. The world's business. If only he could
> find a way out of it.

So you see that negativism in America, while mostly overtly expressed
by the young, is a product of the whole society, and has been growing
steadily during the last generation. As we face these societal problems, the
"establishment" against which the kids rebel is guilty of its own brand of
negativism . . . a much more silent, sophisticated kind. One of the aspects
of this negativism on our part has been our unwillingness to change our
structure and our surroundings to meet the needs of the twentieth century.
We clutch vainly at the things of the past, and caustically dismiss our critical youngsters as immature or as "hippie-creeps." And gradually, as their
voices grow less meaningful and their criticism has no effect, they become
more negativistic and more harsh and thus seem even more unrealistic to
us. So we entrench ourselves even more and we in turn sound even more
unrealistic to them. The result is that a great chasm has grown in America
between the alienated young and the minorities on one hand, and the
moneyed, established, and secure people on the other hand. And on both
ends the negativism is continually growing.

A perfect example of what is happening to America is the 1968 elec-
tion. One of the candidates was the ever hopeful and optimistic Hubert
Humphrey, whose brilliance and good humor as a United States senator
helped the United States meet many a crisis. But in 1968, when Humphrey

began his campaign on what he called the "Politics of Joy," his words fell on deaf ears, and even raised much hostility, particularly in the young. Humphrey found out the hard way the tremendous negativism that pervades the society.

Another example of the national state of pessimism can be found in one of the most popular musical plays of this era: *Hair*. Let me quote a few lines from the central song of the play:

> *"We stop, look, at one another*
> *Short of breath*
> *Walking proudly in our winter coats*
> *Wearing smells of laboratories,*
> *Facing a dying nation*
> *A moving paper fantasy*
> *Listening for the new told lies."*

The most significant pall has fallen on the college campus. Alexander Heard, the President's Advisor on Youth Relations, recently submitted a report to the President. Let me summarize the frightening content of that report. Large numbers of students who would normally be moderate and conservative have become antagonistic. He quotes a University of Minnesota regent as saying that "we find among our bright, hard-working, ambitious, well-read students a widespread distrust of their government, a growing despair about the political process, a mixture of fear and resentment toward America's leadership." Mr. Heard further concludes that "the self-identification of college students as a separate class in society is assuming extraordinary proportions." The most important source of despair found by Heard in his extensive interviews and surveys was the apparent ineffectiveness of our institutions in solving the great problems of the day. Heard believes a most urgent note is required in meeting this pessimism growing in the college students who are the leaders of tomorrow.

Today, America's biggest problem has become the "problem problem." The most vicious part of the problem problem is that it leads to divisions and hostilities that keep us from solving the difficulties that led to the problems in the first place, and as the problems continue unsolved, the negativism in turn gets worse. We are in what could be correctly labeled a "vicious circle" of events.

Let me point to some of the sick things that accrue from the vicious circle of negativism. The first aspect is that instead of "emphasizing the positive and de-emphasizing the negative," we do just the reverse. We dwell upon our problems so much that they seem so disproportionately large and overwhelming that the resultant tendency is to avoid them. An example of this is the tendency by the American media to dwell upon student dissent and magnify a small demonstration completely out of proportion.

Another sick result of negativism is that it creates problems even when there aren't real ones. A perfect example of this was a strike leader, who purportedly contended that he really was not that familiar with the reasons for the strike, and that if one issue had not been at hand, he would have found any other convenient reason for striking the university.

I often get the feeling when talking to the most entrenched student radicals today that they do not want things to turn out right, nor do they want improvements made. They are good and practiced at opposition and contention, but they are completely out of their element in construction or improvement. Negativism, you see, has become a fashion at colleges and universities. What started out a very legitimate ethically based protest against overly paternalistic and rigid university rules has now become discontent aimed at not only every real problem of the society, but every flaw in human nature. Student radicals today blame every human problem inherited through the centuries on the "establishment" and the "system." Once these false correlations begin to be acceptable to a student dissident, his negativism has become a sickness.

As negativism has become a sickness, undermining reason, we have lost track of a fundamental fact of human life in the United States. I am speaking of the fact that things are not really so bad as they seem. There is evidence that many things are substantially improving. Fortunately, I don't have to rely solely on my own interpretation. My points are corroborated by the text of an address given by Daniel P. Moynihan, Counselor to the President, at Hendrix College, on April 6, 1970.

Mr. Moynihan said, "The fact is that in our eagerness to draw attention to problems, we do frequently tend to make them seem worse than they are. In particular we tend to depict things as worsening when in fact they are improving." Mr. Moynihan cited the example of race relations. The University of Michigan Survey Research Center recently disclosed that "the white backlash and the deterioration of white and black attitudes toward integration, which have been noted by many social observers, do not show up in the findings of a recent Survey Research Center nationwide survey. There is evidence that in some respects, blacks and whites are in closer and more friendly contact than they had been four years earlier." Moynihan further points out that over the last years a variety of different programs, criticized though they may be, have both helped millions of deprived and disadvantaged people and have even more importantly set the precedent and gained the experience to help millions more in the coming decade.

Another example with which everyone in this room is familiar is the continuing improvement of the working man in the American society. The benefits of an affluent society have been in the last years ever more evenly distributed to the millions of working men across the society who have made this country and built what we consider its heritage. In education, fantastic progress has been made not only in the kind of teaching done and the material being taught, but in providing the opportunities for more and more students from all backgrounds to attend colleges and universities.

Let me summarize my remarks. Our society has problems; there is little doubt about that. Some of these problems are serious. These problems have emerged largely because we are a nation in great change. We are a young nation going through the process of maturing. We have been a rural nation and we are now becoming an urban one. We have been an expanding nation and now we have reached the time of internal consolidation. All of these throes of history are natural and understandable, but in America growing pains have suddenly become a tremendous national crisis. For a variety of reasons, a historical movement of negativism has emerged into our period of consolidation and not only prevented the solution of many problems, but at this point threatens our very well-being. Before any of our societal problems will be solved, we must first solve this problem of negativism.

I recommend that the first move to conquer this state of depression take place where the responsibility for directing the society lies: in the hands of those in positions of social and political power. A hand must be extended to our kids. Not an ingratiating hand, not a patronizing one, nor one that plays to their passions. We must move as a society to take the words of our young seriously. We must integrate them into our society's positions of responsibility. They must be made part of the process of our educational and political institutions. The channels must be opened all across our country to permit constructive and practical outlets for our youths' admirable humanistic goals. I see the first steps in this direction being taken by our universities in integrating students into the policy-making councils. I see other steps being taken in allowing eighteen-year-olds to vote. I see other moves in encouraging youths to campaign for candidates. These changes and a thousand more like them can turn the tide of negativism into a positive movement to humanistically develop American society.

At the same time, we must resist pandering to coercive and destructive attempts to further drag our society into a no-man's land of hang-ups, problems, and psychoses. A healthy society cannot be built by bowing to unhealthy passions and demented misperceptions of reality. What I am painting here is a very delicate balance that must be reached, and it must be reached soon, as Presidential Advisor Heard has documented. We don't have much time to clear our fog of negativism and begin the long-postponed solutions to our society's problems. History, we know, will not wait long for us.

The Democratization
of Higher Education

BUTTERWORTH HOSPITAL SCHOOL OF NURSING GRADUATION EXERCISES

GRAND RAPIDS, MICHIGAN

JUNE 1971

I WANT TO TALK TO YOU TODAY ABOUT A TREND THAT IS SWEEPING higher education in contemporary America. I call this trend the "democratization of higher education." This trend embodies the greatest changes that have faced higher education since its inception in Colonial America. I want to talk about this trend both because of the tremendous impact that it has for everyone in this society, and also because it substantially involves the medical professions.

American higher education is facing the demolition of what has most commonly been called the "ivory tower." For years in America, higher education was not a right dispensed by the society, but instead was one of those not easily attained values in American society that could be afforded only by persons with a relatively high income.

Another characteristic of higher education in past years was the atmosphere within a college. Students faced a system known as "in loco parentis." This meant that higher education was considered by students' parents as not only a time for educating, but a time for growing up. Students spent four years growing up before they were faced with the real world and its problems. You probably remember as well as I do the old college fraternity songs telling of the hard cruel world waiting outside the university and how the graduating seniors were going to conquer that world once they emerged from the university. But the world, you see, was something *outside* the cloistered walls of academia.

Higher educational institutions thus became responsible not only for the knowledge that young Johnny or Mary absorbed, but also for their morals and their ethics. Students were considered as growing children whose activities, ways of thinking, and ways of life needed as much supervision as their themes in composition class. That advice was freely given, and in past years gratefully received, usually with a minimum of backtalk.

A third characteristic of higher education of the past was the quality of the academic life on the college campus. The adjustment to barriers of academic attitudes was as significant as overcoming the barriers of wealth. Classroom material and subjects discussed were often related as little as possible to the outside world. The academic was a search for abstract truth and the watchword of education for generations was that education needed no other justification than to be "an end in itself."

This traditional way of viewing education became an ideology for those who existed within the ivy-covered walls. The college campus in America over a period of some hundreds of years became one of the institutions in society which was most resistant to change.

New and innovative ways of dealing with academic material were looked upon with great suspicion. Practical and professional scholarly activities were likely to brand the participant as second class academic citizens. It is probably not going too far to say that every attempt was made to protect education from the realities of the outside world.

These three characteristics of higher education in past generations may have had their advantages particularly at the time, but eventually they led to the stagnation of the educational milieu. The times and the college-age generation changed radically, but the American university was slow to respond to these stimuli from outside academia. Alienation and frustration grew, legitimate attempts at change were blocked, the danger signs were ignored, and the situation erupted.

The most noticed criticism of higher education was that of the students, because their acts of rebellion against the system were both overt and dramatic. The focus of attention being on the students, there has been an underestimation of the fact that students' parents have become as critical and as seriously disconcerted with the educational system as their children. Taxpayer and legislature rebellion regarding education is at least as serious, and will probably have more implications and consequences than all of the student revolts.

One of the most important, and in a certain way amusing, aspects of the current distress regarding higher education is that the students on one hand, and the taxpayers and legislators on the other hand, feel great animosity toward each other and somehow have come to imagine that they are on opposite sides. The fact of the matter, however, which will be noticed as the emotionalism dies away, is that they are very much in the same camp. The students' criticisms that have resulted in disruptions, sit-ins, and take-overs are very much the same kind of criticisms that have resulted in frustrations on the part of citizens and legislators.

Let me explain these widespread complaints:

1. There is a common belief that faculty members do not teach enough to undergraduate students, and do not pay enough attention to the students' individual and academic needs. This is a well-founded complaint on the part of both students and their parents. Over the years, we allowed a system to develop, generally known as "publish or perish." This meant that it was more important for a professor's future to publish than to teach students.

2. College students and their parents share the criticism that there have not been enough educational alternatives for students in our nation's colleges and universities. As our modern society has expanded and developed, it has demanded new skills and new occupations. Our colleges and universities have been slow to adapt to these changes. They have been reluctant to pursue new and innovative programs that train the personnel needed for the twentieth and twenty-first centuries.

3. There is a shared complaint about the antiquated and unnecessary roadblocks that are placed in the paths of students' educational progress. It is believed by many that educators may be deliberately setting obstacles in the path of progress by demanding that every stu-

dent, no matter his interests, background, or accomplishments, should take the same kind of courses, learn the same kind of things, and pass the necessary acid tests in order to finish his education. The need, in general, for various kinds of education has become so important in the outside society today, that we can no longer afford to put test obstacles in the path of a student to see if he can clear them.

4. Students and their parents complain that education is not available enough to all segments of American society. Again, this is a very justified complaint. It is not just a ghetto-based black youth that faces this situation, but the housewife who at age thirty-five desires a higher education, but encounters difficulties because we have discriminated in favor of students from ages eighteen to twenty-five, and against students who are over thirty years of age. Yet it is obvious that the fast pace and technological developments in the nation demand that education become relevant to students of all ages who have the ability and motivation to pursue learning.

5. Most importantly, the overwhelming cry of dissident students as well as dissident parents and legislators has been that the higher educational institutions have insulated themselves from the realities of the outside world. Correcting this difficulty has become a central policy of the Department of Health, Education, and Welfare, and is the foremost concern of almost all state legislatures across the country.

All of this dismay with higher education has had its effect and while it is sad that it took a crisis of these proportions to stimulate change in higher education, it is at least rewarding to find that change is now coming. Each time that a crisis of this kind has arisen, the American system has adapted to it and responded with the changes and modifications that are necessary to preserve the social and political fabric. The result of this adaptation is what I call the democratization of higher education. Let's talk about what I consider the three major overwhelming changes in the democratization of higher education.

1. There has been a universalization of higher education. Today education is being made more available to American citizens of all ages, all

classes, and all incomes. Special programs, modified admissions policies, and innovative teaching techniques are being established so that education can be available to all members of the society who have the inclination and ability to learn. This is an important step forward in ensuring a stable democracy in future years. A well-known tenet of democratic theory is the necessity of an educated citizenry. The citizens of a democracy must understand the industrial society and political system in which they live if they are to take advantage of it and endorse the allocation of values that takes place.

2. There has been a maturation of the educational environment. Students in the 1960s have demanded that they be treated as adults, and that they share the responsibility for the decisions of our society. Higher education in the 1960s has found that it has not the resources, the responsibility, nor the right to attempt to control the social and ethical values of its students. Students want to discuss, participate in, and become acquainted with the problems that lie outside the university walls. In this sense, the university has attained its proper place as a stimulating and participating institution in the American society rather than a cloistered hall severed from life's realities.

   All across the country, dormitory hours and college rules regulating social, political, personal, and religious life are being modified. Higher education is ready to accept that an eighteen-year-old student is a rather mature and responsible person. We have found, at the college where I work, as most colleges and universities have, that the students who participate in these important policy-making councils are as level-headed and responsible, if not as experienced, as the faculty and administrators.

3. There has been what I call a "practicalization" of higher education. Theory is being made relevant to practice in many fields of academic inquiry. Bridges are being built between the concepts that are examined in the university classroom and the results that these concepts have in application to the political, social, and economic world outside the university. Increasing validity is being given to professional and career-oriented education. Today, the society outside the university demands that firefighters, brick layers, and auto mechanics be as

skilled and dedicated as engineers, doctors, or lawyers. Modern life demands excellent plumbers as well as excellent college professors.

America is a service-oriented society, and all of the services from medicine to firefighting are becoming equally valuable. Material rewards have also kept pace with the increasing status of occupations of all kinds throughout the nation. In case you haven't noticed, plumbers now make a lot of money.

The changes being undertaken in higher education in America are affecting every field, and the medical fields are probably being affected as much if not more than the others. Most of you are aware of the pressures that are being exerted nationally for medical and nursing schools to open their doors to more students who can emerge from the university to render the tremendous amount of medical services that are needed in American society. Students with motivation and ability who previously would not have been able to receive medical-related education because of limitations of income or educational background are now being recruited and trained.

Medical-related professions, as the rest of higher education, are also having to face up to the fact that varieties of experience and training are necessary throughout the society. We are rapidly learning in higher education that a student can be a fine water pollution analyst without having a PhD in biology. We're learning that a student can be a fine data processor without having a PhD in computer sciences. Similarly, the medical professions are learning that there are many health activities that can be achieved by persons who are not medical doctors. Para-professional training is rapidly developing. The time that is necessary for accomplishing degrees and levels of health-related expertise is being shortened.

A great outcry has come from society that doctors, nurses, and other health personnel are needed in many communities that are going without proper medical attention. Plans are being developed so that doctors, nurses, and other personnel can be channeled into those sections of the country whose segments of the population most need medical attention. The days where fine medical attention was a result of having achieved some level of social status or high income level is a thing of the past. A modern technological nation dedicated to raising its standard of living for all of its peoples cannot afford this kind of situation. If democracy is to survive, we need not only an educated and aware citizenry, but a healthy one.

And so the health-related professions have been faced by the same democratization tendency that has invaded other areas of higher education. There has been an attempt to make medical-related professions equally accessible to all of the members of the society and to provide the services of the medical professions to all the members of the society. We at GVSC are also engaged in this activity. We are attempting to undertake a Baccalaureate Degree Nursing Program. We have an expanding medical technology program and we are planning and implementing other paraprofessional training such as psychological nursing, bio-psychology, and other professional areas that are needed by the society at large.

It is my point of view that the democratization of higher education in all the fields of activity in which higher education is involved is one of the most significant and revolutionary movements to exist within this country. It is also one of the most necessary for the survival of our nation. I am hoping that as the years of the 1970s pass, there will be a continually upgraded level of education throughout this nation. This will result in increased political, social, and economic awareness on the part of all ranks of our citizenry, and the expansion of previously unrendered services of all kinds for those members of our society who desperately need them. I am proud to be engaged in this trend in higher education, and to see it achieve momentum in my generation. All of you are similarly engaged in this process. It is one of the most exciting times in American history, and I hope that you join me in lending our support to it with all the energy that we can muster.

Commencement Address

GRAND VALLEY STATE COLLEGE
COMMENCEMENT CEREMONIES
JUNE 10, 1972

Yours is the college generation that lived through the end of the free speech controversy and the height of the Vietnam War protest. Through all the tensions on this campus and others, two underlying human drives kept asserting themselves—the individual's need to count for something, to be a factor in the life process, and his need for freedom to be and do what he thinks he wants.

I want to talk about those two drives, how they relate to one another, and where they may possibly lead.

The democratic tradition, the educational system, the instant gratification of material needs, the worship and fear of technology have combined to create in us an intense desire to protect our freedom. This protection has called forth an almost paranoid concern with decision-making processes. Authority in whatever form is always suspect, and we feel we have the right to participate in all the decisions that affect our lives. When we fail to have a voice, a feeling of futility sets in, followed often by cynicism.

In our protection of freedom we are trying to create the conditions in which our lives can count for something. We do not want our individuality stamped out. Each person must feel important, at least important enough to influence his destiny.

In some respects, technology in the field of communication contributes to our sense of futility. It keeps us from seeing clearly how we can affect life by placing us in intimate contact with decisions and decision-makers that are beyond our ability to directly affect. We watch the President of the United States on his visit to China. Daily communiqués keep us posted on his conversations with Russian leaders. We are told that his visits and conversations will affect our lives and we are not participating— just watching. No wonder our feelings of political impotence are increased. We are conditioned to see what the most powerful do, how the best in every field perform, so we believe that what we do and think are unimportant and have no effect.

Add to this the fact that most of us matured at a time when material needs were gratified with relative ease and our problem is compounded. We are frustrated when we cannot see the direct and immediate result of our wishes and actions. We are not patient in ascertaining the ways we can make our influence felt in the best interests of society and for the building of our own self-esteem. As children, when we wanted an ice cream cone, we wanted it now. When we want ego satisfaction, we want it now.

So our exposure to the world beyond our immediate reach and our conditioning to instant gratification of desires conspire against the successful quest for personal identity and a satisfying life. We are a people whose aspirations are high and require persistence, compromise, alteration, long hours of work, and often surrender of some will to achieve, yet temperamentally we want fulfillment fast, with a minimum of effort and no compromise, if possible.

Though the condition I describe is not universal, it leads many people away from identification with national and even community goals. It tends to place them in a perpetual state of dissatisfaction with themselves and others. It feeds the fires of freedom fighting, but to what end—freedom to do what? Even when a large degree of freedom of action and speech is achieved, it isn't recognized for what it is because the dissatisfaction is still there, so the battle for elusive freedom goes on, but not clearly defined.

The quest for meaning, for self-identification, is the crux of the matter.

Freedom without it is like a vapor. Influencing other people is a way of proving that we count, that we have identity. For all people, this must begin on a rather simple level. We must learn to know and care for the people closest to us, in families, at work, in social and political relations. Influencing does not necessarily mean controlling, but it does mean what one thinks and feels has meaning for the lives of others and becomes a conditioning factor in their thoughts and actions. I like the term "getting everything together." "Getting it together" implies getting thoughts and feelings sorted out so that the individual can get together with others, live in a way that his thoughts and feelings influence others constructively, and he in turn is influenced by others. The beginning of self-fulfillment is not the achievement of control in all that affects us, but learning to understand and relate to those with whom we live our daily lives. The people who are most successful at that will be the best qualified to exert greater influence in an ever-widening circle. No matter how wide the circle, whether it be a nation or a family, the successful achievement of gaining for one's self a positive meaning in the lives of others is the ultimate in human fulfillment and identification.

We live at a time when the commune is again in vogue. Though I do not believe it will be the answer for many people, I admire the motivation behind it: people seeking to share with one another, wanting in simple ways to mean something good to one another, to be important to one another. The word for this relatedness and shared meaning and importance is "community." My pitch to you is on behalf of community. In a mobile society, in one that is bombarded by news about where only a few live and act, the most powerful, the best performers, the most beautiful, we as a people have a demanding task to achieve community where we live.

A community exists when each member recognizes his membership. Membership is acknowledged when each member sees his role in the community as necessary. Before people can build a community through effectively filling their roles, many must experience the feelings that derive from good, intimate, personal contacts. This provides the conditioning that makes it possible for individuals to form a healthy group. The group life is community and within it are many roles to be lived in the interests of all. Improvement of education, wise use of natural resources, a climate for fair dealings in business, improved production and sales of goods and services, fair distribution of wealth, adequate facilities for leisure, a fair tax structure, fair racial practices, adequate political administrative structures to operate public business, good roads, good housing, quality health care delivery, pollution control, and other concerns offer everyone an opportunity to fill a role. With an effective role established, the individual will find identity and see freedom for what it really is: the guarantee to the individual of opportunities toward an important place for himself in the lives of others.

The problems that keep people from building community, and those of existing communities, are not first solved in Washington or Lansing. If we look beyond the place where we live for their solution, we are doomed to failure. Help may be necessary on the national and state levels, but the solution begins at home in the way people live together. Most people find their roles there.

The usual commencement address urges graduates to set their sights toward the stars. I ask you to look into yourselves and where you live and build community.

During your years at Grand Valley, the college entered upon an experiment in community. As numbers of students doubled, separate colleges and institutes were formed, each with its own identity and a sense of community. An important aspect of the experiment is whether several college communities with their own identities can feel an attachment to and an appreciation for the larger Grand Valley State College community. In some respects, our campus is a model of social experimentation, for the success of American society will depend on the quality and development of small, diverse communities. It will also depend on whether or not the individual can feel love, loyalty, and importance within the small communities where he lives, and at the same time emotionally transcend his small community ties to give allegiance to a larger social community.

In the past few years, our sense of community has been sorely tested and in some instances shattered. It is tested and shattered by war with its killing and waste of resources, by racial attitudes, by differing values between groups and generations, and by rapid change in life brought on by technology and affluence. As we set ourselves the task of improving our national life by becoming involved in building the communities around us, we can profitably recall Abraham Lincoln's words to the people at a time of great internal strife: "With malice toward none, with charity for all, with firmness in the right, let us strive on to finish the work we are in, to bind up the nation's wounds, to care for him who shall have borne the battle . . . to do all which may achieve and cherish a just and lasting peace among ourselves and with all nations."

I urge you to find purpose and identity in helping people appreciate one another by providing a psychological cement to hold good relationships together. Fight for and use freedom for this end.

Convocation

SEPTEMBER 1, 1981

I AM CURIOUS ABOUT THE ORIGIN OF THE TERM "IVORY TOWER" AS IT IS applied to the college and university. There is an implication that academia is immune from the pressures and tensions of most social and economic enterprises; that somehow in the educational cloister contemplative work takes place and pure truth emerges and is imparted to colleagues and students. There is a further implication that we who devote our lives to the academy are impractical; that we live in an unreal world sheltered from the harsher realities with which normal mortals must cope.

In the past fifteen years, particularly during the Vietnam War, were the protests and riots on campuses less real than in the streets of our cities? Is there something different about broken glass on a college campus and broken glass in a Los Angeles or Newark ghetto? Ask the parents, college friends, and professors of a student murdered on campus how sheltered the academic environment is. The "ivory tower" has tumbled down for hundreds of professors and administrators throughout the country who have lost their positions because of economic recession or decline in enrollment. Arson in dormitories, students threatened by fellow students, faculty and administrators charged publicly with misconduct in a way that

tends to sensationalize and make them appear guilty until proven inno-
cent, are all conditions which have destroyed any immunity college life
had from the harsh and often dangerous forces of American society.

The term "ivory tower" originated, I am sure, at a time when less than
5 percent of Americans enrolled in colleges and universities. Higher education was an experience removed from the lives of most people, though
still influential in the technological, political, and religious direction of the
nation. It was an experience reserved and deemed necessary for only a few.
"Ivory tower" then is not an unusual sobriquet for a place that provided
such an exclusive experience. Now that one half or more of Americans
attend college at some time in their lives, it is not surprising that those who
devote their careers to higher education deal with a greater range and volume of human problems than their predecessors.

Whether or not the "ivory tower" was ever what those who coined the
term perceived it to be, today we know it is not a sanctuary.

Just as "ivory tower" implied a special place apart from harsh realities,
it also expressed indirectly a special purpose for those who worked there.
Though I regret the passing of those easier days when the world was not
too much with us, I am more concerned that we will lose our sense of special purpose as the corroding problems of the modern campus stain the
"ivory tower."

In addition to being appalled by the invasion of harshness to which I
referred earlier, we must listen to and respond to terms such as productivity, market, and accountability—terms foreign to our profession. They are
thrown at us and explained in a manner that offends our sense of what we
are about and increases paranoid feelings towards those outside and within
the university. We try to explain. We argue. We feel powerless. We defend.
We develop positions. We intellectualize. We map out strategies. We want
to preserve what we hold dear. We want to survive. All of these actions
taken for self-preservation more often appear to me to be self-destructive.

The sense of special purpose is endangered by the fears and fights
brought on by economic stringency, closer public scrutiny, and continuing
criticism. We cannot ignore the new conditions on the campus, but the
best way to survive is to hold before ourselves and the public the special
reason for our existence. Without our doing what we have chosen to do,

what we have been called to do, society itself is endangered. If we in the academy lose our vision because we are not tough enough to cope with some adversity, we will betray ourselves and all of society.

The origin of our profession winds back in time to the period when Socrates, and even his predecessors, became preoccupied with human problems. From that preoccupation grew a concern for man's improvement and education. In a simple statement Socrates is reported to have said, "If we want to improve and educate our young, the first thing to consider is what virtue is." Virtue in ancient Greek is a morally neutral word compared to the meaning it has after centuries of the Christian experience. In Socrates' time, it designated excellence—the excellence of anything in any field. As described in Plato's work, Socrates states that whatever is able to do its proper work, fulfill its proper function, attain its proper end or good, we call a thing of virtue or excellence. Socrates never tires of saying "Virtue is knowledge." This is the substance of his moral teaching.

Am I correct when I say we believe as Socrates did? The nearly twenty-four centuries since Socrates have seen an explosion in knowledge. Man continues to pursue knowledge and uses it in pursuit of his self-fulfillment. This is what we call education. The process is one in which we are seeking excellence (virtue) for our lives through our knowing. By knowing we come to deeper understanding of ourselves, others, and the nature of that which is a part of our experience.

What we describe as the mind is the part of each human life that perceives knowledge, excellence, and ultimate meaning for that life. The mind is the receptacle of human consciousness. It is even used consciously to probe subconscious behavior. It provides the means for us to make the religious decisions of our lives. It is the machine of each human life that produces knowledge that finally determines what life for the human being will be. Whether one embraces a loving God who works through the minds of men and women or believes that man shapes what destiny he can in the natural order, the mind is all one has to consciously perceive and know. It makes human life, human life.

Can you think of anything on earth much more important than the human mind? I cannot. In all of life, what priority do you give to the growth of the mind and through it to the increase of knowledge and understanding? For me it's right at the top of the list along with love of family, and securing food and shelter. In fact it assists in the full realization of all other priorities. As inheritors of the Socratic tradition and concern, we, the members of the academy, have assumed as our responsibility the nurture of the mind so that knowledge may be expanded, truth discovered, and the life of man enriched and dignified.

Now tell me again, as I have heard recently, that the state or society cannot afford so much education. We are not dealing with outmoded products that are no longer useful in society. We are dealing with the mind, a limitless, exciting, necessary resource. What we can do for the mind is without limits. The academy, like any other institution, can learn to live with more or less, depending on conditions, but it must live. Once our society has committed itself to the ideal of an educated citizenry, it should not turn back. Knowledge for the many, not just for an elite few, is the new American ideal. It has become part of our national dream. Only in recent American life have we moved towards it. Naturally, its achievement is not complete, nor is the process unmarred by false starts. The goal is noble, and at Grand Valley we are instruments in our own way towards the realization of this goal.

The most serious threat to a college or university comes

- when its members lose their commitment to the life of the mind.
- when those who teach and pursue research have other interests that impinge on their time, keeping them from doing their best.
- when there are distractions of a personal nature or frustrations because the system does not provide a good environment in which to work.
- when staff at all levels forget that they, too, are trying to create a place where learning and knowledge take precedence.

To live with declining purchasing power is particularly difficult for those accustomed to an affluent society. Tension arises over the division of resources. One finds it less tolerable to accept programs and people with whom one disagrees or does not respect. Comparisons of who gets what become odious. There is always the fear that less today may bring even less tomorrow. Such times are hard and distracting. They require hard decisions. Yet those decisions must be made, always considering the responsibility of the academy for the life of the mind.

While collecting my thoughts for this address, the sacred quality of our mission impressed itself on my mind with a renewed force. What our profession requires of us is so important in the lives of the people we serve, it is awesome. Their minds, their thoughts, their decisions, their careers, the relationships that flow from all of these are at stake in what we do with them. When they are not, we lose sight of our mission. We become mired in pettiness and internal power plays, and lack the necessary attentiveness to our most important tasks. We become vulnerable to and deserving of attack from outside. The faculty are closest to the holy of holies of the profession because they deal most often and directly with the students' primary reason for being in college, but that does not detract from the essential contribution others make to build a worthy college.

To enter a classroom, to conduct a class, is almost a priestly act. One has a feeling of that as I did while watching an able first grade teacher lead her twenty-four six-year-olds through their lessons in reading, word definitions, and writing. She was awesome in the simple way she communicated with her students. The same feeling of awe used to come over me in an American History class when the professor day after day presented us with the most literate, analytical lectures I have ever heard. He performed high art. He was immersed in his subject. He loved the knowledge of it. His pride would not allow him to demean his subject or himself. What he taught was lifted to a high place. He and the subject earned stature and both had an influence on his students; he because his devotion and intelligence gave us an example of superb teaching and the subject because it was taught so well and had a richness and complexity that was fully explored. He helped us understand what he wanted us to understand.

Ours is a sacred profession because knowledge is our métier. If we hold with Socrates that knowledge is virtue, there is no more important human endeavor than the extension, understanding, and use of it. Knowledge is comprised of lesser and greater elements. It is incapable of being comprehended in its entirety by any single individual, yet all of it is within the purview of the profession called teaching and research. Each of us in our own way works a part of it. There is no more important profession than the one that deals with knowledge in the search for truth and understanding. We must believe it. More important, we must practice it worthily. Finally, we must explain as best we can the nature of our work and its consequences for the future.

Ours is a sacred profession because we are involved in a force that shapes the future for individuals and society—the aspirations of our students. We encourage them or discourage them. We help them to see themselves realistically. We open doors to knowledge so that they may achieve their goals. We are drawn into their lives when they face decisions and work towards objectives that will have an ultimate effect on who they are and what they do. There is a frightening aspect to this responsibility. Clearly each class and counseling session is significant because of whatever effect it may have on the direction of a student. Each administrative system that injects itself into the life of students may alter attitudes, hence the way a student may go.

For the past several minutes I have shared with you my view of our profession. I have done so because ours is one of the worthy, noble professions of humankind, and we are going through a difficult period. Last year the economic disaster made these the most trying times of our young institution. No institution lives through retrenchment and reallocation happily. No college or university will survive a difficult period unless its people have a sense of the worthiness of their profession as educators, and through all vicissitudes hold to that ideal.

Here we are at the beginning of a new year. There are 2,500 new students with their hopes still intact. They are not conditioned by the threat of Tisch amendments and 14 percent budget reductions. They are placing their aspirations in our care. We will summon the age-old commitment of the scholar to his discipline, to his institution, and to his profession and immerse those students in the life-inspiring process of education. We will treat their minds with reverence. We will reward their success, but we will not tolerate indifference or indolence towards that which is precious, even sacred, to us. We will be renewed by all of this. We will live and take pride.

As we enter this academic year with new students, with returning students, and the commitment we have to them, we should hold before ourselves a few objectives that will help us to be a strong institution in these times. Quality, after all, is determined primarily by people—their thoughts, their work habits, and their dedication to task. I do not wish to imply that books, equipment, travel, and facilities do not affect quality. Yet all of these can be provided, and without the will and intelligence to use them, they will not make a strong college or university. In these days all of us can give careful thought to how we can improve what we are doing. The Committee on Research and Development is available to assist those who conceive a formal plan to contribute to the scholarship and teaching of our institution. A better lecture, greater intellectual involvement with students, a good article, cutting of red tape, solution of a problem in an equitable manner, make for a better place. To improve in these ways may do more for a college than costlier additions. Is it possible for each of us to dedicate ourselves to doing something better this year than we have done it before?

This summer there have been discussions with the Committee on Research and Development about recognizing teaching and research excellence each year. This was done to call attention to the purpose of our profession, to honor what we are entrusted to do, and to honor those who do it particularly well. Awards would be presented at the Opening Convocation. Discussions are underway also to find ways to appropriately acknowledge superior administrative and staff work.

Two years ago I asked that an all-colleges general education program be considered by the faculty. Actions taken recently by other colleges, including Harvard and Stanford, indicate that the request was timely. I am aware of the conflicts amongst our colleges on the acceptance of credits. Yet it seems to me scholars and teachers bent on excellent education and broadly educated students can find a way to identify the areas of knowledge to be included in such a program and to establish the means to see that the quality of instruction is acceptable to all. To fail in this endeavor is to fail as an institution of higher education. To build a coherent general education curriculum in the pluralistic, professions-directed university today is a major challenge—one that educators must meet for the good of the human mind and the professions themselves.

Recent times have brought us unforeseen retrenchment and some necessary reallocation. In some ways we have become more efficient; in others we feel the loss of what was cut. I do not foresee the immediate need to retrench positions again, nor is there any reason to threaten the existence of our four fine colleges. We must continue, however, to pursue ways to increase our effectiveness academically and financially. Last year we combined some functions formerly in two or more units into one. We should examine our operations to see if other combinations are in the best interests of the Grand Valley State Colleges or any one of the colleges. This, too, is an area of potential conflict, but we cannot avoid it.

Grand Valley found financial support from the private sector since its beginning. The land for the campus, Seidman House, WGVC-TV, Loutit Hall, and the Stadium Track are all examples of projects that relied on private support. Our future depends on even broader participation by individuals and private organizations in our fundraising campaigns. The Board of Trustees of the Grand Valley State Colleges Foundation has been expanded for the purpose of increasing our endowment fund and securing a downtown center. Our alumni, our friends, and all of us will be asked to make what contribution we can, and we will seek out new friends as well. What we are doing here is important for this region and for the state. We will see that we continue to do it with state assistance and, we hope, increased help from all those who recognize our significance.

Here we are together again. All the problems thrust upon us have not disappeared, but neither have the opportunities. We will have to deal with the problems, but let's dwell on the opportunities. If we think together and keep communication open, we may find creative ways to help each other enhance our colleges. I invite you to talk with me any time about any subject. I hope you will return the invitation and extend it to all colleagues and students.

Socrates talked about virtue and knowledge. He also talked about wisdom. Wisdom is the ability to discover inner qualities and relationships. Wisdom keeps knowledge working in the best interests of the human race. Wisdom is knowledge's safety valve. Wisdom is common sense. Knowledge by itself is not wise. The way we use knowledge, the way we perceive relationships, the way we act toward people is wise or unwise. The success of these coming weeks and months will be determined by how much accumulated wisdom we have around here. I trust the supply is sufficient.

Lakeshore Chapel Sermon

AUGUST 15, 1982

HAVE YOU EVER ASKED YOURSELF THE QUESTION, "WHAT'S AT THE end of the universe?" That question hardly pushes itself upon you during the busyness of everyday life. What's at the end of the universe is not a pressing issue when there is food to be cooked, money to be earned, relationships to sort out, and all kinds of health considerations. One of the difficulties about the question if we do ask it is that we really cannot answer it except with an answer like eternity, or black holes. These are answers that require explanation we cannot provide.

If we are honest with ourselves we must admit that it is impossible for us to give rational content to the concept of "never ending," just as it is impossible to accept the fact that eventually the universe has a boundary, and beyond it is nothing. If that's the case, nothing becomes something. It really is a rather tricky question. What we come up with when we pose the question is an acute awareness that our minds are able to probe and think about dimensions that it cannot yet grasp or explain.

We have been taught that we are made in the image of God, but we can't quite replace Him or Her. Most people deal with this question as much as they deal with their own mortality. They have faith. They believe that what is beyond our consciousness has order and meaning, and is ultimately good because it is in the nature of things and God is at the heart of the nature of things. There is reality, and we see part of it, but we believe strongly in the reality of the part we do not see.

Before wheels and boats and written language, I wonder if people ever thought with a sense of mystery what was beyond the great mountains that loomed above them, majestic and impassable in so many parts of the earth. There have been so many questions that at first cross the mind. Sooner or later they obsess some people. They live with the questions. Finally, through hard work, using the mind, some rather complicated and complete answers emerge that in turn lead to more questions and more answers. Life has been an evolving process for Homo sapiens from the time we first appeared, unable to write or maybe even speak except in grunts and screeches. No matter how much feather bedding of ideas or obscurantist thought, the questions come and the answers follow, sometimes faulty, but often with some truth that leads to new vistas of understanding.

There is a theory, appealing to me, that consciousness as we understand it developed over a period of time, that man was man before he was conscious of the fact as we are conscious of it. My discussion this morning will assume it to be fact, fully recognizing that some communions would consider such a statement heresy. Fortunately, I cannot be defrocked since I am not a minister. Freedom of speech is guaranteed in our Constitution, so my only risk is that of offending some of you, which I would regret. To those whom I might offend, I will not offend long for this is not a long sermon.

There is no doubt that man existed before written language. The development of a sophisticated language is evidence of a developing consciousness and the use of that language, both linguistic and mathematical, propelled the rate into more communication, greater discoveries, deeper knowledge, a more highly developed sense of what being human is, and an awareness of the future possibilities of knowing. This process does not come evenly throughout the earth, nor has it eradicated brutality or what we call inhumanity. Our expectation that life can and should be good, our belief in the possibility of human goodness, causes us to label the brutality inhuman. We are concerned, even worried, about this failure of the race to live in peace and understanding. Why has it always been that way? Our religion, which is the expression of what we believe and need, has provided content and structure for us to reach our highest aspirations for the human spirit, but too often it contributes to the misunderstanding and animosities that lead to our warring. Religion becomes an intermix of our best and our worst.

Our strong beliefs often compel us to act in ways that change and improve the human condition. They also bring us into confrontations with those who believe just as strongly what we cannot tolerate. Sometimes the confrontation leads to better understanding, sometimes to conflict, sometimes to understanding after conflict, and sometimes to continuing conflict.

In our religious experience we can reflect on the teachings of Christ. When I read the accounts of what he said, I come to the conclusion that he was trying to free people from some limiting religious and social ideas and structures. He didn't condemn all; he gave new perspectives. Those new perspectives have not been lost. They gave and give people a higher consciousness of their own value, and a different concept of God. Yet man has also used Christ to fashion limited religious and social ideas and structures. Perhaps the problem is that some people are just limited in thought and spirit or have a grasping need to control all that is a part of their lives, even the ideas of others. More than that, they cannot live with ambiguity or their own lack of knowledge, a condition all of us must live with.

After all this discussion, what I am saying is that these steps in human experience that lead to more, new, and better insight do not lead to unmitigated goodness. Better is not always the best for everyone. People can take what is good and mold it into something that is not. Advancement in human knowledge and understanding of the universe, and specifically that part that is human nature, does not always bring immediate improvement for everyone in spiritual life, philosophical insight, or economic circumstance. But it makes a difference because life for man has changed. The birth of a child in Bethlehem, the manufacture of a sail, the carving on the Rosetta stone, harnessing electricity, the printing press, a man named Plato, breaking the atom—all of these have changed life, have improved life, even though on occasion they have been used to destroy and dehumanize it.

When we look back to the earliest evidence that man exists and compare *Homo sapiens* then and now, we cannot deny an unusual progress in all fields of knowledge. This evolutionary track has not carried goodness exclusively, but man knows more and has continuing potential to break through to greater knowledge and understanding if the past is a mirror for the future.

I wonder at what period and across whose mind the question first flitted, "If I could fly, how fast could I travel?" When that question was first posed, did it seem as impossible to answer scientifically as the one I asked, "What's at the end of the universe?" Remember, too, it is less than five hundred years ago that people of considerable intelligence thought the world was flat.

We have reached a stage where we are beginning to probe outer space and measure time. We have ideas based on research about the life of a star, even a galaxy. Put in that perspective, we know what a short period of time is filled by the human experience on earth. For me, that makes the human experience all the more impressive. To see the development of consciousness and the increase of knowledge through consciousness in such a short period of time compared to the life of our galaxy, the sun, or the earth, leads me to believe that the next five thousand years provide the possibility for man to live in dimensions that are hard for us to conceive. Whether or not he will know what's beyond the boundary of the universe, I don't know, but he probably will have expanded those boundaries. One of the interesting prospects about death is the possibility of more dimensions of experience beyond. We live in a three-dimensional world with beginnings and endings and color. We are aware of that at an early age. A cow lives in a three-dimensional world with beginnings and endings and no color. She is not aware of any of that. She lives on the same earth, but she cannot fully comprehend our world, though we live side by side. Is there a fourth or fifth dimension, or a quality of life that we are blind to, that we do not comprehend; dimensions and qualities that are within the province of God? I don't know whether cows know more now than they did five thousand years ago, if there were animals then resembling cows, but man certainly does. He is now conscious of dimension, and knows infinitely more than his ancestors. That is why I believe what lies beyond man and in the province of God is open territory for discovery and settlement when man is ready and has the will for it. We are made in God's image in so much as we know and understand.

What I have tried to do is analyze the human condition and the process of human life. From that analysis I draw certain principles, which one might call doctrines, religious principles, or canons. You have all heard of canon law in the Catholic Church. Canon law comprises rules for church and religious life. I choose to call mine the Lakeshore Canons. They will not make a big explosion.

Number one is "Keep the Faith." Belief has been the engine for survival and progress for the human race. Belief has caused bloodshed. It has been and is mistaken. It is also a comfort and, I believe, often a right understanding. Martin Luther and John Calvin used the concept to address particular theological problems in their time which still have relevance. My particular brand of faith is a belief that man's seeking will lead to useful discovery, that what we do not know may be known for the enrichment of man and therefore to the glory of God. I believe that human life is sacred, and must be treated with dignity and respect. When it is, the conditions are right for more discovery and understanding. Man must believe in himself and the worthiness of the life given him. There is some evidence that faith has worked in the past, but that is no guarantee for the future. One's belief in the future is faith.

Number two is "Think Rationally." One does not have to believe that rational conscious thought is the only means to understanding or knowing. Much extra-conscious machinery was installed in the species long before consciousness became an overriding characteristic. Having said that, I will contend that most trouble in the world emanates from man's failure to use the power of his reason. Rational thought is the best means we have to continue our quest for knowledge, the best means we have to understand ourselves.

Rational thought is a demanding master. It keeps you honest with yourself. To betray it is to betray your mind, your brain. It may not be the fount of all truth, but it makes you examine what you believe and why you believe it. Without it you become the victim of impulses and theories that play to hidden needs without restriction. The bad consequences of good discoveries and insight can usually be traced to the breakdown of reason, and the rampage of emotion unchecked. The knowledge explosion and its consequent opportunities for the species was and is impossible without it.

Number three is "Respect Mystery." Reason may unravel mystery, but there is always more that is unknown and mysterious to be unraveled. What we don't know, yet anticipate, holds us in awe. At least it should. Those who do not respect mystery usually lack humility. Their sin of hubris is a sin against all that is, and all that is to be learned. It is important to accept ourselves as unknowing at times.

We must be aware of and respect strong and deep feelings that we cannot yet understand, that our reason has not or perhaps cannot penetrate. To respect mystery, however, is to respect also the human process that has replaced mysterious explanations with scientific understanding. What was mystery to an ancient, something that to him was for the Gods to hold in secret, is for us often a rationally explained phenomenon. Respecting mystery, then, is to be grateful for the route and distance we have come and it is to be respectful of our and our progeny's future journey. It is also to bask in the wonder, love, and joy of life with understanding it all.

You have heard my three Lakeshore Canons. That is enough for today. After all, we have to play on the beach, eat lunch, and look for those boundaries at the end of the universe!

Humanities for
Business and Society

CONFERENCE AT STEELCASE
OCTOBER 19, 1983

WHEN ONE CHOOSES TO SUPPORT THE NECESSITY OF THE HUMAN-ities for Business and Society, an opening quote from Plato, Aristotle, or perhaps Machiavelli, Thomas More, or Shakespeare would be most appropriate. I am not going to do that. But to maintain my own reputation as one deeply interested in Humanities, I want to assure you I have not neglected their works this past season, but I must confess that at present I am swept along by the mass of America's reading public doing my part to catapult James Michener's latest volume *Poland* to the top of the best seller list. From that work I quote the fictional Polish Count Lubonski, who is addressing both a Lithuanian and a Ukrainian colleague:

> To justify becoming a nation, the land and the people must have produced a unifying culture. By culture I do not mean folklore, cooking patterns or nationalistic myths. I mean music which all respond to. I mean architecture which constructs buildings of spatial and utilitarian importance. I mean conscious poetry, not doggerel. I mean great novels which

generate and define a people's aspirations. And above all, I mean the creation of a philosophy which will underlie all acts passed by your parliaments, all utterances made by your teachers and professors.

Gentlemen, the accumulation of such a culture requires time and the dedication of men and women who know what they're doing. (Here he paused, almost afraid to make his next statement. Then, walking briskly back to face his visitors, he spoke.) You Ukrainians have not had time to build such a culture, and if you try to establish a state of your own with inadequate foundations, it will collapse. Vondrachuk, I assure you, it will collapse, probably within ten years, because you lack the cohesive background upon which to build. You lack the music, the architecture, the beautiful town squares, the great novels. I concede, the poetry you have, thanks to one man who would understand what I'm saying, your fellow Shevchenko, who almost single-handedly gave the Ukraine a soul.

There are many elements necessary to construct and preserve a society within a nation. Nations do not survive well, if at all, without a strong economy and either military power or military protection from a military power. But I agree with the fictional character Count Lubonski that there must be a culture, a human condition linking people in some common bonds before an acceptable national society can exist. Feelings, values, perceptions of life and reality reveal themselves through literature and poetry, music, philosophy and religion. These are the avenues through which the thoughts, emotions, and feelings of people are made into a heritage, and they also become the system of values that sustain and protect that heritage. These are often varied and contradictory, at times diametrically opposed, but they must exist, be a part of a society before a modern society can exist, certainly before any group or groups of people can be a nation.

I will make the extreme statement that a society cannot survive or at least be remembered as a society unless it has or leaves a record of its humanistic expression. In the past it has been the humanistic contributions of one time that have linked it to another and it is through humanistic expressions that one period has influenced the future. What we call

the Humanities have been until our recent industrial, technological revolution the major distinguishing characteristic of human species. Religion,
philosophy, music, art, and literature have communicated what being
human is. They have revealed the species for what it is.

Count Lubonski made a good point, I thought, about the necessity of
a deep, developed, and varied culture for a national society, but you
remember he was doing so to persuade the Lithuanians and Ukrainians,
who had different problems, to join Poland so that there would be military
and economic power sufficient to sustain a national society. That's the
other side of the coin. If one comes to the conclusion that well developed
humanistic expression is necessary for a society to be called a society, or for
any long-term national life to exist other than a propped up travesty of
national life, then one must ask under what conditions can humanistic
expression best be developed. Certainly freedom is quickly put forward,
and undeniably freedom is helpful. Yet the literature, music, and art of
Russia, and even more recently the Soviet Union, has distinction, deals
with the depths of a people, and comes from a society never noted for the
kind of freedom we hold to be inalienable. No, it flourishes best when
business, commerce, and agriculture sustain more than subsistence living,
when education is encouraged whether the society is elitist or democratic
in its approach, and when there is enough power to preserve at least for a
period of time a relative stability. The stability gives rise to increased commerce, and though interrupted in the past by wars, the commerce leads to
greater wealth. Depending on the distribution of the wealth, a culture can
develop with a high level of humanistic expression.

Not always have the philosophers and artists of a culture expressed
themselves or been interpreted in ways that led to peace and a higher level
of civilization. Yet the best in civilization, according to our values, has
always been accompanied by a high level of humanistic expression and
active commerce. Successful business is one of the best ways, if not the best
hope, for providing a civilization in which man can probe most successfully
his own nature and the perceptions and ideas that flow from the probing.

When free to soar under any circumstances, the pursuit of the
humanities leads the species to greater self-understanding and insight,

and can (but there is no guarantee) enhance those conditions under which a stronger economy can evolve. The humanities are necessary for business and society just as strong business in a stable society is the foundation for the pursuit of humanistic study. The question is almost a chicken or egg one.

After talking a rather long time to spin out my rather simple and easily attacked theories on the assigned subject, I conclude with a few categorical statements about what we should do to encourage the humanities in our society which has already developed a rather high culture despite what some in countries with a longer history might say.

1. A democracy to survive in the future requires a high level of human understanding from its citizens. This is best provided on a formal basis through the educational system. At present the level of understanding or sensitivity to literature, art, music, etc. varies widely according to family background and environment. Each school district should assign to an appropriate person or persons the task of assessing the receptivity of all its students at all levels, and design the kind of programs in humanities that will encourage the indifferent to gain interest, and the sensitive to increase understanding and to see how that understanding will apply positively in whatever their pursuits.

2. To single out the study of foreign languages for special mention is appropriate because our nation does so poorly in that field. There is a failure in our business community to comprehend its need for more people who can speak the major languages of the world. We not only must understand others in a shrinking world, we want to do business with them in a way that our economy will be strengthened. Knowing other languages is essential for both. I believe the advocates for language study should be found in the schools as well as the marketplace.

3. Studies in the Humanities for business executives are provided by many colleges and universities throughout the country. Such programs have proven themselves successful in improving executive performance. More can be done on the local level. Schools take courses on technology, management, finance, economics, etc. into places of

business. There may be advantages to the employer, and society in general, if on occasion literature, history, art, and even music became a part of the on-site curriculum in our local business establishments. Who knows what quality of attitude towards self and others might improve our common life.

President Arend "Don" Lubbers addressing students and faculty from the entrance of Zumberge Library during the Vietnam War crisis, circa 1971.

President Lubbers speaks to a student assembly, circa 1972.

Chairman of the Board of Control and founder of Grand Valley State College
L. William Seidman and President Lubbers at an academic convocation, circa 1974.

Vice President of the United States Gerald R. Ford and President Lubbers walking across campus during the vice president's visit to Grand Valley shortly after his appointment in 1973.

Lubbers delivering the commencement address in 1978.

Groundbreaking for the Eberhard Center, the first building constructed in Grand Rapids, June 1985. From left to right: *Fred Meijer, Chairman of Meijer stores, Paul Johnson, Chairman of Grand Valley's Board of Control, Grand Rapids Mayor Jerry Helmholdt, State Representative Thomas Mathieu, Michigan Govenor James M. Blanchard, President Lubbers, University Faculty Senate President Jacqueline Johnson.*

President Lubbers addressing the university community, presenting an agenda during difficult times in the economy in 1980.

President Lubbers speaking at the annual Enrichment Dinner honoring donors to the University, circa 1983.

On a visit to the City of Sarajevo and the University of Sarajevo in 2001, President Lubbers was made an honorary citizen of the city. Here he is receiving the certificate naming him an Honorary Citizen from the Mayor of Sarajevo.

President Lubbers with Provost Glenn Niemeyer and Vice President Matt McLogan testifying before an appropriations committee of the Michigan Legislature, circa 1995.

Nancy and Don Lubbers being recognized and honored by the Michigan Senate for their service to Grand Valley State University and higher education in Michigan in 2001. From left to right: *Senator Glenn Steil, Lieutenant Governor Richard Posthumus, Senate Majority Leader Ken Sikkema, Nancy Lubbers, Don Lubbers, Senator William Van Regenmorter, Senator Leon Stille.*

President Lubbers responding to the students who gathered in the Fieldhouse to present him gifts and wish him well in retirement in 2001.

Retiring President Lubbers greets his successor President Mark Murray, former Treasurer of the State of Michigan and a Vice President at Michigan State University, in 2001.

Don and Nancy Lubbers at their retirement dinner attended by 1,000 people from the west Michigan community and friends from all parts of Michigan and throughout the country in June 2001.

Address to Detroit Economic Club

FEBRUARY 13, 1989

Y OU HAVE LISTENED TO MY DISTINGUISHED COLLEAGUES FROM OUR two largest universities. Along with Wayne State, ably led by David Adamany, the activities at these three important universities claim the largest share of time and space when the Detroit media covers higher education; they, therefore, are likely to be more securely fixed in your consciousness unless you have a personal tie to another college or university. The microscope provided by sports writers alone allows us to peer more deeply than we want into the lives of athletes and coaches at large universities and keeps those institutions prominently in our minds. In Michigan there are ten additional universities and two branches of the University of Michigan. You read and hear about them some, but unless you attended one of them or have been affiliated with one, you may not have a precise vision of what they do for our society collectively or what each does separately. They are as diverse as the landscape of Michigan itself and rather strategically placed throughout the landscape. Each has developed its own mixture of academic programs, yet together they offer the citizens of the state a comprehensive curriculum, designed to deal with the complexities of a modern society and the global economy that drives it, and for the most part this curriculum is well taught. In the late 1960s a presidential candidate claimed to speak for the silent majority in our nation. Today I represent what may appear to all but holders of the purse strings a more quiet majority in Michigan public higher education.

Combined, the twelve institutions for which I speak enroll 139,947 of the 250,933 students in public universities in Michigan, or 56 percent of the total. Equally, if not more important, 70 percent of their alumni are living in Michigan. They tend to have a high percentage of graduates remain in the state—entering business and industry, teaching in the schools, working in the health care field, designing products, starting new businesses, and serving in the public sector. Add to these numbers those who had some education and training, but did not complete a degree. In special fields most directly related to the economy, engineering, and business, these universities have 101,000 graduates working in our state and we estimate that nearly 60,000 of their alumni are teaching the future generation in Michigan's public schools.

These are important figures in the economic life and social fabric of our state now and for the future. In a speech in Chicago last year, the futurist John Naisbitt said, "Contrary to what you've heard, the middle class in the United States is becoming larger and more affluent. And that's true as we shift all over the world to information-based economies." There is not, throughout America, the loss of high paying jobs and a disproportionate increase in low paying jobs. Between February 1986 and February 1987, more than three million jobs were added to the American economy. 41.5 percent of the jobs were managerial and professional. 46 percent paid more than $28,000 annually. Last year 52 percent of the new jobs were managerial or professional. New low-paying jobs are under 5 percent of the total increase in jobs. Michigan is part of this action, as our Governor frequently points out.

The citizens of our state consciously or subconsciously demonstrate an understanding of the phenomenon. How? By going to college. They know what they need in order to be a successful part of this changing economy. Do you remember when experts were predicting and planners were preparing for a substantial decrease in students at our universities? They didn't predict the effect a changing economy was going to have on people's perceptions of the education they needed for success. A higher percentage of high school graduates sought a university degree, now between 55 percent and 60 percent, each year and increasing numbers of older adults flocked to university campuses to retrain for the brave new world. In Michigan, where did they go? To the community colleges and the public universities. Our state ranks ninth among states in the percentage of its population who seek college-level education.

Looking at the numbers and towards the future economy, what are the universities' responsibilities, particularly the ones I represent today?

First: We must provide access to higher education for students of all ages whose work qualifies them for admission. As we enter the next millennium, I believe the numbers will swell. We will begin to see the results in many of our high schools of the reform insisted upon by parents and employers. When we contemplate the numbers of the African-American and Hispanic populations, we know that more of the young from these groups will find the aspiration and the skills to seek a university degree. The nation and this state cannot afford another outcome. The conscience of each public university requires that it encourage this aspiration and insist on the development of these skills. At the same time, there will not be a decrease in the aspiration level of the white population.

Second: The universities must provide a curriculum that leads their graduates naturally into satisfying positions in the new world. Here we need to step up the interaction between the university and the professions that make up our economy and society. I will be surprised if a wholesale restructuring of university curricula is required, but the closer academe comes to those who work the vineyard, the more likely changes will occur in the way the university prepares people for the vineyard. Because of the cost of higher education, we, the professionals responsible for the universities, should find ways to discard what is no longer needed, alter when necessary what is, and hold fast to that which is essential for high quality learning and research.

Third: Each University has a responsibility for research and public service. In the past, little was required in the way of research from our public colleges and universities except from the major research universities. The need to compete in manufacturing, the demand for sophisticated information systems, the complexity of local government, all keep the telephones ringing and the fax machines gorging and disgorging at the smaller universities. The major universities should be encouraged and protected as they pursue basic research. The regional universities will have to take on more of the applied nuts and bolts research and consulting that emerges from the business and industry in their areas because the majors cannot do it all and proximity has its advantages. I predict that each university will increase as a center of expertise in some fields related to its area's economy, and many universities will continue to find ways to link themselves to one another, sharing information and talent as they help propel Michigan's economy forward.

With 70 percent of our graduates remaining in Michigan, combined with those from Michigan, Michigan State, and Wayne, we represent the largest source of our state's professional and business expertise for the future. We as a group are one of the major players in Michigan's future. How well we do our job will be one of the important factors in the state's success or failure.

Early in the nineteenth century Napoleon said, "Public instruction should be the first objective of government." If our Michigan economy is to succeed, we had better make public instruction, kindergarten through the university, a high priority. First, the people have to believe it, then the leaders will. Second, the schools and universities have to deliver what they promise in pedagogy and research. People are willing to pay for what they must have, and we in education had better provide it. Presently we may be in a period where making our case is more rather than less difficult.

First, there is taking place a demystification of higher education. As more people enroll in universities, the more familiar they become. Weaknesses as well as strengths are exposed. There is more disappointment along with the increase in success. People are better able to evaluate and are less in awe.

Second, universities, like all institutions, do not change easily. They are likely to respond initially to new conditions and demands in a negative or at least fumbling manner. This is not universal, but frequent enough to hurt our case.

Finally, the decline of socialism and the welfare state manifests itself in a strange anti-tax movement in our country. As these sentiments work their way through our society, the demand for lower taxes and the desire for services still needs a reasonable resolution. That is the climate in which we live as we speak to you today.

As a Council we share with you today a proposal we have made to enhance our universities so that we may help minorities fulfill their aspirations, so that all who should be educated in our universities will have a place ready for them, that the curriculum we offer will prepare them for what you have to offer, and finally that we will be engines of our economy where business and industry can seek the assistance they need to propel them forward.

In the last decade, state appropriations have not kept pace with inflation. Buying power from state dollars actually decreased by 4.5 percent. Currently we rank thirty-first among the states in appropriations to public higher education as a percent of tax revenue and twenty-sixth in appropriations per student enrolled in public institutions of higher education. This is not where Michigan used to be. To accomplish what we believe we must, we are suggesting that the state consider appropriating to the universities each year for five years beginning in 1990 an increase equal to inflation plus 3 to 3.5 percent. We then would be well on the way to recovering what we lost in the devastating recession, and preparing for the tasks of the next century.

Our objective today is to raise your consciousness about Michigan's public universities. Combined, fifteen of us, we are a three billion dollar business, yet we are a fairly independent lot. Of all the states, we are the free enterprisers of higher education, each with our own Board of Control, but we are coming together to bring Michigan effectively into the twenty-first century. As the cooperation level improves amongst ourselves, we seek also more cooperation with you and those you represent. We need to know what you think we should be doing. We need a compact for Higher Education—a compact between business, industry, and higher education so we educate the right people for the right places, so we work on the right problems.

Linking education with the health of the state and the economy is an ancient concept. Diogenes said over 2,400 years ago, "The foundation of every state is the education of its youth." We can expand that to include all the people in our modern state. By working together, you can keep us alert and more effective, and we can give you worthy women and men to build on your heritage.

Lakeshore Chapel
Sermon

AUGUST 13, 1989

SINCE THE DAWN OF CIVILIZATION, PEOPLE HAVE NOT BEEN CONTENT TO see events as unconnected and inexplicable. As their lives were affected by events, they insisted on knowing the causes. And their gods to whom they assigned the responsibility for initial and ultimate cause reflected the environment in which they lived and the degree of knowledge they had acquired. Originating in their concept of a divine intercessor or intercessors came the systems, some primitive, others evolving into complex theologies, that provided the explanations that connected events and experiences into meaningful life.

For primitive tribes the gods were locked in the animals and plants that gave them life, and totally comprised their environment and occupied their minds. Throughout history God made the rain fall, and gave food in abundance or withheld it. The strong arm of God gave victory or, by assisting the enemy, brought defeat. Before the age of science, the sacrifice of lambs, fatted calves, and young unspoiled youths placated the Gods and brought the desired effect. We have all seen rerun movies where some high priest stands with a knife or sword poised to slaughter, in the name of his religion, some beautiful young virgin, only to have the more civilized warrior, who obviously came from a society with better theological understanding, snatch her from imminent death, carry her away with the implication that she too will share his more enlightened understanding, as well as their marital bed.

Our own Judeo-Christian faith is rooted in the same traditions, the same kind of explanations of the human condition. When Abraham, to satisfy his God, Jehovah, was about to sacrifice his son Isaac, Isaac was snatched from the jaws of death, not by some swashbuckling adventurer, but by the voice of God. When the experience of civilized humanity reached a point of understanding the futility of blood sacrifice, and that the forces for good and evil existed within men and women neither aided nor abetted by the blood of animals nor their own blood, they postulated that God was willing to be the sacrifice and by so doing forever meet the need that all previous blood offerings had fulfilled—and, by overcoming death through resurrection, allay that overriding fear of death more successfully than humankind had done through all manner of belief and practice heretofore.

Built on the ancient Judaic perception of life, the new Christian understandings captured the mind of western man, and for more than 1,500 years dominated the frame of reference in which people found explanations and meaning for their lives. By the seventeenth century the drive to discover and know had led to the firm establishment of those physical and natural theories that led mankind into the scientific age. The new science had and continues to have a profound influence on how we think about the explanations Christian theology has given over the centuries about the nature of God and the meaning of life.

Humankind's elemental drive to know and explain has a contradictory aspect. One of the most noted novels by Joseph Heller, written in 1961, was *Catch-22*, about a U.S. airbase in Italy during the Second World War and an airman, Captain Yossarian, who found himself in innumerable impossible situations. What he was ordered to achieve always undermined the achievement. Sometimes it appears that the species' drive to know and explain is humankind's catch-22. Scientific knowledge provides information that often undermines the current explanation that has been offered as "the truth" in explaining the nature of God, the nature of man, and the nature of the universe. A new ultimate truth is formulated until the drive to know and explain offers up more information that tends to undermine aspects of it. So our compulsion to know has led theologians, philosophers, and common people to systems of belief explaining all phenomena relating to life and death, and then that drive to know, in a generation or more, pushes them, not all at the same time, to question the systems that were constructed. We fear the unknown, yet we tend to plunge into it, and by so doing come to know more.

The compulsion to know has led Christian scholars and leaders throughout our religious history to explain in detail every aspect of human life and death, the world of nature, and the nature of the God who is behind it all. Let's examine some of the areas of explanation that have been unsuccessful and those that continue to serve us well.

During many years of reflection I am not sure I have found a satisfactory answer to the question, "Why in our Christian tradition do so many believers and theologians feel compelled to explain phenomena in terms of what they *want* to believe, and then defend their explanations when there is reason to re-examine them?" It is only five hundred years ago that Copernicus put forth the theory that the earth was round, a concept that went back in history as far as Aristotle, but had not seen the light during the dark ages and the Christianizing of the west. That concept, along with the removal of the sun and the earth as the center of the universe, was so vigorously opposed by the church in the sixteenth century that its most celebrated proponent at the time, Galileo, had to recant in order to remain alive. No matter how much the keepers of truth or the Vicar of Christ on earth proclaimed that Galileo was wrong, he was in fact right. I believe the "big bang" theory of the origin of the universe causes difficulties for some people because it makes their perception of God the creator antiquated. In his book, *A Brief History of Time*, Steven Hawking, the noted British physicist, and a genius of our time, helps those of us who are laymen attempt to understand where the discoveries in physics and astronomy are leading us. The possibilities of the universe he describes transcends the earth-centered universe of former Christian theologies, and the understanding of modern day scientists. Yet these new paths to the future are often blocked by people who say, "Don't mess with my God!" Maybe that's the problem. We like to claim God. We want to know what we think God does, he does; what we think he is, he is; the need to know and explain is impatient.

In my home city of Grand Rapids, controversy over the Biblical story of creation is causing a stir, and has spread throughout a conservative denomination. The battle is fought over whether or not the earth was created in six days. People are being attacked and maligned over the issue. I see nothing ennobling or enlightening about the controversy. To me it is unimportant, except that the passion with which a really scientifically untenable position is held leads to the deterioration of personal relationships and deals a blow to those who espouse good will.

In the political realm as well, the drive to know and to be right is used to cover man's aggressive side and his drive to power. Wars in the name of truth are as familiar to us as the daily soap operas—Protestants against Catholics in Northern Ireland, Muslims versus Jews and Christians in the Middle East, and a few years ago Catholics fighting Buddhists in Vietnam, the Thirty Years War on the continent in the sixteenth century where Catholics and Protestants started what continues today in Northern Ireland, Cromwell and his pious round hats against the Church of England, and the Catholics in Ireland. The litany is endless. I am sure when you are involved the reasons seem justified. But to the outside observer they appear to be a miscarriage of what religion ought to be.

During my many years of reflection I have come to some conclusions. First, one should not confuse religious truth with his or her views and understanding of the universe. This understanding should always be open to new discoveries. Second, one should not believe absolutely anything that has not been observed. That does not preclude holding positions on subjects that do not lend themselves to observable verification. Those positions should be intelligently put forth and just as intelligently altered or set aside if observable evidence leads in that direction. My conclusion is that most of the positions we take should be held with humility. Our minds are awesome in their ability to think, reason, understand, and give us our consciousness. That awesome ability brings new discoveries in science and reasoning that transcends and changes the level of knowledge previously attained by the human brain. Therefore, the very mind with which we believe has the capacity to provide new insight and enlarge the belief. That is the reason for holding what we believe in humility. If we do so we are not at sea in intellectual chaos, yet we are open to ideas and thoughts of others that may enrich our lives. This is easier to do for some than for others. The ancient force from within to know and explain in certain terms is part of our condition. Often it leads to intolerance and an intellectualized ignorance. If laced through with humility and a gracious willingness to understand that our knowledge is only a step to knowing more, the primal drive to know and explain serves the species by increasing insight and understanding in the nature of life and death, and avoids the pitfalls of round after round of energy-sapping argument and strife. At best the argument and strife is verbal and unrelenting. At worst it takes its toll in human life.

The vigor with which some of the theologians, rulers, and populace at large intertwined their views of the universe, using what is now discredited science, with their religious views of the nature of God, was not in most instances a useful exercise. A little more humility and tentatively held beliefs would have meant less blood spilled in the name of religion. Furthermore, it would have carried with it less exclusivity that each religion claims for itself, and encouraged more sharing and less killing.

While religion has been an inadequate guide to scientific truth, and often made to look ridiculous when insisting on views that are not consistent with proven scientific theories, it has been successful in identifying and developing beliefs about human relationships that give purpose and understanding for human life. Our Christian faith, for instance, has some profound insights that do not ensnare us in battles over scientific discoveries.

We begin with the concept that God enters man through Christ; that the spirit of God is available to everyone. There is no need to appease God with the sacrifice of life. There is the opportunity that the spirit and power of God can move in and through every individual. Christ speaks of the God within you. "I am in the Father, you in me, and I in you." Over centuries of experience people came to understand the power of love, and that to live in a state of love, acceptance, and forgiveness with those around you was to live in harmony with the spirit of God. It was the highest human fulfillment, and not in conflict with scientific discoveries or practical human achievements. The New Testament specifically states that God is synonymous with the spirit of love. Those that shut themselves off from it are weakened, even lost, in their ability to find and understand what the essence of fulfilled human life really is. The worst human condition is the incapacity to love. Without the capacity to love, the individual is shut off from the spirit of God within. With it the spirit of God dwells in a person, and generates the power to improve human life and make it worth living.

Our religion speaks of all life in reverent tones. The animals, the trees and plants, the grains of the fields, all of nature has value and dignity. In furthering respect for nature, religion has never come into conflict with science. Nor has this insight been altered when other strongly held beliefs have finally given way to overwhelming scientific evidence. Where religion has succeeded, the drive to know and explain has been in play. We have thousands of years of experience with the effectiveness of love and the ineffectiveness of hate. We have observed what love does to lives. The Christian religion and other religions are based on that experience and observation. We can believe it with certainty. We know it and we even explain it.

We have always been a part of nature. Our stories of creation speak to that fact. Though we have not always lived in harmony with our natural surroundings, and at times have suffered because of nature's forces, we are aware that the natural environment and we are part of the same creation. We are aware that there is a harmony to be found in man's relationship with nature. This we are learning with greater intensity and insight, but the concept has always been central to religious understanding. And in our need to know and explain, people have continued to examine the natural order of life and the universe. In our search, whether looking out beyond the stars or into the smallest particles of matter, we find order, cause and effect, a meaningful unfolding. The scientist is awed by the vastness of what appears to be nature's plan and the student of religion is reaffirmed in his or her faith that life has meaning.

In our need to know and explain, let us be scrupulously honest. We do not need to appropriate a claim to all knowledge as if we were God. We are better served to admit to an honest uncertainty, to qualify what we are inclined to believe with the possibility that we may discover more. What is learned about the universe, and much is being postulated, will add to or change our concepts of our creator. What we learn about matter and energy may alter our views about the human species and its relationship to nature. This exploration is part of our drive to know and explain and will not threaten sacred cows if we don't keep the cows around. We may even find out how many angels can sit on the head of a pin, and end the fruitless arguments about the subject.

So much theological discussion seems to me like working out a puzzle—entertaining, but of little significance. We should be more discriminating in our religion about what we really know and what we only think. We know the power of love exists and is the most God-like force in our lives, and we know that we are part of a natural order of life that has harmonies and explanations available to it. That is really enough to know absolutely. To open ourselves to discoveries that may bring in their wake new ways of viewing our religion will only add to the wonderment, spiritual growth, and joy of our lives.

Address at University
of Sarajevo

JANUARY 10, 1990

I AM HONORED TO BE INVITED TO ADDRESS YOU TODAY ON THE OCCASION of the University of Sarajevo's fortieth anniversary. My first visit to this city was in 1951 and subsequent visits to the university and Sarajevo over the past fifteen years attest to my strong appreciation and affection for the people of Sarajevo and my colleagues who comprise this distinguished university.

I must remind you scholars in attendance at this symposium that our American system of higher education allows a President of an American university to remain in office for so long as he or she can survive. I have been a survivor for nearly thirty years, and I enjoy the work of an administrator. The price I pay for that enjoyment is the time required to pursue a scholarly field. As a consequence these brief remarks about the mind of the twenty-first century are not based on legitimate research, but are the opinions of one who works actively in a mid-American provincial setting to keep his university current and pointed in the right direction as it moves toward the twenty-first century. Those opinions may be peculiarly American, but of course that is what I am—a Midwestern American—and I share with you thoughts that spring from the ground and intellectual climate where I have been nurtured. That ground is not quite so isolated as it once was just as the lands on which each of us trods are bound more closely together and the earth is becoming a collection of neighborhoods. I believe, therefore, that there is some legitimacy in speaking about the mind of the twenty-first century rather than minds of the twenty-first century because people throughout the planet are likely to become more interactive and more interdependent, though not necessarily more agreeable, less competitive, nor ready to act in the best interests of themselves and others.

In their first issue of the New Year, one of the United States' news magazines, *Time*, selected Mikhail Gorbachev as the man of the decade. Of course, some Americans disagreed with *Time*'s choice, but I am not one of them. In fact, I believe he may be the man of the century, even when compared to one of my favorites, Winston Churchill, or to Adolf Hitler, whose energy, neurosis, and peculiarly self-centered view of history unleashed more destruction on the human race in a shorter period of time than that wrought by any previous warrior or disease. Stalin, Lenin, Mao Tse-tung, and Roosevelt are other candidates. Perhaps a scientist should be selected in this most technological of centuries, but for now I go with Gorbachev, because he understands that individual freedom of thought and expression will be the "bed rock" for any truly successful society in the future, and he had the courage to act politically on that understanding. Others in Eastern Europe had the same beliefs and were pursuing them. When he acted, the "freedom cat" was out of the bag, and one of the mental preoccupations that will continue into the next century was openly identified. How to govern democratically will be the question asked by people throughout the world. Democracy, government structured to reflect the will of the governed, will be on the minds of people now and in the twenty-first century. There will be few if any societies where the issue will not arise, and every autocrat and oligarchy will have to contend with the movement towards democracy.

The issue of democracy will be raised with intensity and force. Whether or not it will become the standard form of governing in the twenty-first century is an open question. That question will be answered in the twenty-first century, and the quest for that answer will be one of the consuming issues of the time. In nations with no or little tradition for democratic government, will the growing freedom amongst the people carry with it the discipline and sense of justice necessary to sustain democracy? In free states, the transition of power is peaceful or the freedom is lost. In free societies, people live through economic difficulties without violence or the surrender of their freedom for a quick economic fix.

In Eastern Europe, the transition taking place has a heartening aspect. With the exception of your neighbor, Romania, the bloodshed has been minimal, and there are many who can claim some of the credit for this unexpected response to demonstrations that were unusually peaceful. I surmise that some formerly in power and others who led the opposition are responsible for this step towards civilization. And of great importance was the temperate speech and careful politics of Mr. Gorbachev, not only for Eastern Europe but for the response elicited from the countries of the west. In Romania, where blood was, spilled the desire for freedom, intensified by what was happening, became so strong that the beleaguered people of that nation were willing to pay the price. Can anyone question that freedom and democracy are foremost on the minds of Romanians these days?

What roads will people follow with their new freedoms? Will ancient grievances and attachments to tribe and ethnic group be stronger than the desire to live in a pluralistic, multi-ethnic society? If they choose the former, will freedom survive; will ethnic enclaves function in a global economy? Can the diverse interests of people living within the present national boundaries be subsumed by the will of people to live in freedom, a freedom that can only survive if everyone is ready to give as well as take? That is much easier for a homogenous country such as Japan and even Hungary than it is for the Soviet Union.

In the United States we have a history of freedom and democracy in a multi-ethnic nation. Our democracy has survived a few constitutional crises and the endemic corruption that accompanies human greed. Most Americans have commitment to and experience with democracy, and personal freedom is our unassailable right. On this planet we are old hands at it. But we have our challenges. Our freedom makes us more vulnerable to excesses that a totalitarian regime can limit more easily. The phenomenal wealth of the drug cartel depends on a market. We practicers of democracy, in part by virtue of our freedom, have the wealth to provide the drug dealers with customers. And we in the United States are doing it to the point of national peril. Crime, decrease in productivity, and sapping of moral energy are a plague and, in the long run, if not abated, will threaten the freedom and undermine the democracy. If such decline were to set in, the answer to the question, "Where is democracy in the twenty-first century?" will be different for the world than the answer will be if the United States keeps its moral fiber. Another dilemma our old democracy faces in a world that is and will become more intent upon that form of government is illustrated by the United States' recent invasion of Panama. That the dictator was the most unsavory of rulers, that most Panamanians rejoice at their deliverance from him, does not make it a favored way to bring about the transition of power. I support my government because Noriega should not be permitted to brazenly exploit his people nor threaten others with his drug involvement, but I regret the means that reminds us of days past. The irony is particularly poignant when such profound changes seem to be taking place in Eastern Europe.

The extent and health of democracy and freedom in the world of the twenty-first century will depend on the development and success of a global economy. Another feature of the twenty-first-century mind will be its interest in and concentration on matters of international economics. Economic considerations have played a major role in wars of the past. Economics and world trade may become the war itself in the future. The shift from the desire for territory to the desire for markets may accelerate in the twenty-first century. Winners and losers may no longer be determined on global battlefields, but on world markets. War is too dangerous and when it erupts, world powers will be more inclined to keep it localized. The exertion of power, the satisfaction of egos, and the thrill that accompanies action may well be directed to the world economic sphere. There is ample opportunity to be aggressive, even nationalistic, in economic matters so that those tendencies when necessary can be exhibited there rather than on military fields of battle. We can hope that this will be the case, not only to spare human beings death and destruction from war, but because it offers opportunities for win–win situations. With the absence of major wars, the peaceful economy of the globe can provide an increased standard of living for all who will actively participate. If people can use discipline in their national economies, a beginning will be made towards a more healthy global marketplace. The "if" is a big one, but the rewards in the future are so great if this is done; the 1990s will reveal whether or not the national will exists within enough nations to accomplish this end. Whether it does or not, the twenty-first century will be the century of the global economy. What we do now will determine if we enter the century as an economically happy or unhappy world.

Where I come from, the fax machine is replacing the postal service for all but mass mailings. In time everyone's telephone will have a fax machine or its equivalent. Computers in phones will permit common data to be used and manipulated by people at the same time in locations distant from one another. Already we can see each other and talk with one another anywhere in the world if the proper equipment is available. Soon we may be conducting symposiums with you by communications satellite. At my university, we have the equipment and are beginning to do just that within the United States.

The technology is available to put several book volumes on a microchip to be read on the screen of your personal computer. The problem arises from legitimate copyright laws, and the present financial incapability to provide at least each scholar and student in the world with a personal computer. Think, however, of the long-range implications. All journals may be stored in computer banks to be drawn on throughout the world. This is being done in some fields, and of course wide bibliographical data is available through this means. Books so difficult to secure in many countries will be pulled out of a computer bank half a world away. A book on a chip the size of a fingernail can be copied and distributed. All this can be done, and in the twenty-first century a way will be found to "do it worldwide." A golden age of worldwide scholarship is coming with the communications technology revolution. The younger generation will adapt to the means better than most of us and, as they do, our professions will be transformed. In the meantime I will always touch with reverence the hard covers of the books that I read in bed each night.

The minds of the twenty-first century will be occupied for some time with the role of women in the professions and women will agonize and

disagree, but they do and will have a place different from that in any previous century. Men will struggle to understand themselves in relation to
the new territory women will claim for themselves. From my background
I am unaware of the role of women in different societies. Only my own is
familiar to me. When I am in Yugoslavia I am aware of the important role
women have in the University and even in the government, but I have
everything to learn about the subtleties of this important topic in your
country.

Stimulated by more education and pushed by the need for two-family
incomes, women are in the professions to stay. In the American Association of State Colleges and Universities, there are nearly four hundred universities enrolling more than half of the nation's students. The majority of
those students are women. In the United States 52 percent of all college
and university students are women. Not only do they compose the majority, but at my university and the majority of universities the women are
proving themselves as a group to be better students. Sex aside, quality will
of itself eventually prove decisive, and women will match and exceed men
in academic performance. As the majority of women university graduates
enter professions, many jobs held previously by males will be passed on to
females. What this will do in professional and personal life is subject for
another paper. Certainly the excitement of new frontiers to conquer that
are now open is stimulating women in our society to excel. Many men surrendering a psychological worship in their profession as well as jobs are
unsure often of what to do. The twenty-first-century professional will have
this very much on his or her mind, and early on this will be an even greater
preoccupation than now, balancing career and parenting, and safeguarding
the rights of a woman in her profession who chooses motherhood along
with her job. And one of the great choices in the later twenty-first century
will be whether or not a woman will carry her own child or have it in a test
tube and incubator. The century will bring greater changes, opportunities,
and choices for women than ever before, and the male response to these
inevitabilities will be equally important in the determination of the harmony and quality of human life.

There are many changes "blowing in the wind." Some have been
blowing a long time, as far back as the sixteenth and seventeenth centuries.

The church, both East and West, as guardian of the truth in matters relating to life on this earth and in the next, felt the first winds in the west when disagreement so intense caused the Reformation and a counter reformation to purge and cleanse. A stronger gust came with scientific discoveries from Copernicus and the scientific minds of the seventeenth century. The eighteenth-century thinkers carried the implications of the physical scientists' discoveries into the social, political, and economic spheres. When the antidotes to the evils of the ancient regime, with its close alliance between the keepers of the truth and the keepers of the state, reached the refinement of nineteenth-century thinkers, most notably Karl Marx, organized and even unorganized religion was left in the "dust bin" of history. Of course that did not lead to the demise of the church, but in Eastern Europe and later in China, areas of vast population were officially discouraged from or prohibited from the practice of religion. In much of the west, particularly in the twentieth century, the church no longer dominates the world view, but is a retreat and assurance for the faithful and an anachronism to large numbers.

Dostoevsky said that man will insist on worshipping something. Now we see that the antidote philosophy of Marxism, even with its significant insights, may have overreached itself in its claim of understanding more than it did. There are many throughout Europe and North America who are ready for an in-depth evaluation of values and their source. I wish I knew more about the climate for such an examination in the Far East and Latin America. The rigid orthodoxies that protect peoples' identities still play a major role on the world scene. They are part religious, part political, part ethnic, and part psychological. They will fade slowly if at all. They range from individually helpful to politically destructive and they are not the future. The twenty-first century is waiting for those open minds who know that there is no final revelation, but building on the best of what was believed and the experience of those who believed it will seek to gather more insight into the life of the spirit and the nature of the universe. They may find their understanding in an old structure that transforms itself or outside the formal structures established to tend the values and the mysteries. It will not matter. The success or failure of life in the twenty-first century, however, will depend on people finding values in common that will help them relate in spirit as they pursue their more temporal interests. They can come from the alienated or the devout. They can draw from past tradition or new insight, but what they find must be performed in order to effect and save life. These matters will be important to the mind of early twenty-first-century people in North America and Europe at least, and the quality of the understanding of those who engage will determine how important the life of the spirit will be throughout the century. In turn, the quality of life on the planet will be determined by it.

What an agenda we in the universities have! Charged as we are to lead in matters of the mind and I believe the spirit as well, let us take upon ourselves the responsibility for a constructive playing before our societies the important issues in political choices, economic development, the technological revolution, the role of the sexes, and search for values. I think my later years hold more interest than my earlier ones. The issues are so grand, the risks so great, and the potential rewards a vision for living.

Lakeshore Chapel Sermon

AUGUST 12, 1990

"**A**LWAYS REMEMBER THE WEAK, MEEK, AND IGNORANT ARE ALWAYS good targets." This is from an internal memo to Lincoln Savings Loan bond salesmen. A Secretary of Housing and Urban Development watched soaps on TV while his rich-girl executive and her pals doled out HUD dollars to their already rich, obviously greedy, friends. When asked if his money had influenced United States Senators, Charles Keating, Chief of Lincoln Savings and Loan, said, "I want to say in the most forceful way that I can, I certainly hope so." Leona Helmsley, often referred to as the Queen, commented that "only the poor pay taxes," and took tax deductions for personal non-tax deductible expenses. Every six minutes a woman is raped in this country. Motorists who don't like the way you're driving on a Los Angeles freeway are apt to fire a gun at you. A TV personality mock-sings the National Anthem, spitting toward the flag, and grabbing her crotch during the singing.

Is there something amiss in the land? Have we reached a point where the United States as a nation is at moral risk? I am usually an optimist. I prefer to motivate and inspire by positive reinforcement, but I am a realist too, and I want to share my concern about the moral climate of our nation.

What characterizes the moral malaise in a society? Certainly, as in all moral breakdowns, "self before service" is the major theme, and the theme manifests itself in human behavior through greed, lust for power, sloth, cynicism, and violence. These are human tendencies that social institutions are designed to hold in check, and the process of their development and the success of their function is what we call civilization. They have been successful enough for the survival of the species over the millennia, but not so completely successful to shelter people from pain, disruption and decline of their cultures, distress, and often early death.

If any of these characteristics—greed, lust for power, sloth, cynicism and violence—dominate a society beyond the point where it can be thwarted, the society will inevitably decline. For a nation to be delivered from the destruction inherent in any of these qualities, citizens must think and behave right. For that to happen, right thinking must be defined and opinion mobilized in support of it. The cause, then, is carried by an institution or institutions valued by significant numbers of people and personal, as well as public, behavior is modified. The process is never perfect nor the results absolute, but they pervade enough to insure the survival of the society until the next time. Public morality and public policy and action flowing from it are dependent on a shared concept of personal morality.

The American people, both before and after establishing a nation, have looked to the traditional institutions of church and government to check the destructive tendencies of humankind, who through the practice of religion and law attempt from time to time to purify themselves and renew the society.

In American life there were three major periods of spiritual renewal when moral weakness was perceived to undermine the well-being of the land. The Great Awakening, lasting from the 1730s through the 1750s, was fueled by the conviction of men like George Whitefield who preached outdoors to crowds of twenty thousand people. A burst of missionary zeal and zest for social justice unleashed new focus in the colonies. Here began the earliest drive to ban slavery, as well as a movement for prison reform.

Societies were formed to feed and clothe the needy, provide for widows and orphans, and set up dispensaries to treat the sick. Higher education was encouraged and Princeton College opened as a direct result of the revival. Many scholars believe the Great Awakening led to a political liberation that directly contributed to the American Revolution. Jonathan Edwards, the noted New England preacher of the time, writing about Northampton, Massachusetts, where he lived, stated, "There was scarcely a single person in the town, old or young, left unconcerned about the great things of the eternal world. Those who were wont to be the vainest and loosest, and those who had been most disposed to think and speak slightly of vital and experimental religion, were now generally subject to great awakenings."

The second period of revival and renewal came in the early national period from the early 1800s to the Civil War. The coarse life on the frontier was partially responsible for its origin, and Kentucky and Western New York State were cockpits of religious fervor. People would come for hundreds of miles to camp meetings where itinerant preachers like Charles Finney speaking to crowds up to twenty-five thousand in number sought to transform society by saving individual souls. Finney's advocacy of disinterested benevolence was paving a direct highway to the abolitionist movement. And it was the abolitionists who finally forced the issue to end what is surely the greatest moral evil in American history—slavery.

The period between 1890 and 1917 can be called the third era of revivalism. To contemporary Americans some of the objectives of the movement—temperance and Sabbath observance—do not strike a responsive chord, but close observation shows how important they were as forces for social change. Temperance leaders like Frances Willard urged women to take their moral power outside their homes to influence society at large. The campaign against strong drink was not a narrow moral issue, but recognition that it was leaving women and children destitute, breaking up homes, and leading to domestic violence. Women were on the march, and their new spirit not only carried the nation into the unsuccessful experiment in prohibition, but gained for them the far more important and lasting right to vote. The crusade for Sabbath observance touched the way Americans live and was practical as well as religious. Recognizing that laborers often worked sixty to seventy hours a week, calling for Sabbath rest was a form of labor legislation.

Our history, then, reveals the capacity of the American people for renewal. I hope a head of steam can build up for a fourth era of revival. Certainly the conditions call for it. The greed is evident. Charles Keating, Ivan Boesky, and Michael Milliken are shining examples. They and others are on a road to uninhibited self-gratification. Misusing people, their resources, and the law all are incorporated in the modus operandi of the greedy. Even with their downfall they leave damage beyond measuring such as the S & L scandal.

We have a collective greed too. We are a nation of citizens who want services and safety, but are unwilling to pay for them. Our Congress and Executive offices have a history of failure in financial management. Who is to blame? We are now beginning to eat our seed corn because we are not willing to curb our appetites or buy more corn.

The lust for power is always with us. Donald Trump might qualify. George Steinbrenner, the baseball and shipping magnate, has the characteristics. The lust for power is the overriding need to dominate, control other people's lives, make them always bend to the will of the power holder. If they don't conform absolutely, destroy them. In the long run, it doesn't work.

Sloth: The slothful gobble up the seed corn faster than anyone else. Look at the welfare dole that pays more to stay home from work and have babies. Look at the unemployment that encourages people to stretch the law to the limit and beyond so that the able-bodied can be paid while not working. Sloth weakens the economy and character.

Have you ever observed anything more cynical than Mayor Marion Barry giving talks to children on clean living and saying "No" to drugs while smoking and snorting as much cocaine as he could get his hands on? No matter what the verdict, he is a shame to the human race. A strong society exists only if there are shared common values. Behavior like Barry's is truly cynical because it undermines the teaching of necessary values. What child can believe anything positive if Barry was once his or her model? A pervasive cynicism prevents foundation building for a society.

And violence: Our nation is the murder leader of the world. Violent crime and the sexually deviant behavior that often accompanies it appear to be a "made in America" product. Many of our citizens are injured daily by mindless drug-infected people who mask as wild animals. The injury and loss of life are only part of the evil. The mind of the person who perpetrates such crimes is often impervious to persuasions that could extricate him from his condition. His spirit is dead, and there is no spark that can ignite it.

I think there is enough evidence to declare a need for spiritual renewal. But in the past the appeal was made to a nation of enough shared values to rekindle a strong sense of moral purpose based on those values. Is there too much diversity of experience today, or is the moral vacuum too great to elicit a response? That is a possible problem. Yet we should not be deterred because the challenge appears formidable. America is resilient and must have renewal.

To whom should the modern day George Whitefields, Charles Finneys, and Francis Willards address their message, and where will they come from?

There are two groups of people in our population that are of particular interest to me. The first needs hope injected into their spirits and moral information into their minds. They are mostly poor, but not necessarily so. They are usually without benefit of positive family life or minimal good education. They tend toward amorality if not immorality. They are more likely to act without thinking, to be substance abusers, and to satisfy untempered instincts. They don't disbelieve so much as they disengage in belief altogether. They often have psychologically inflicted wounds that they do not understand, yet determine their behavior. They are a vast underclass, and they are our greatest national problem.

I am reminded of the excitement for missionary work created by past revivals. The revival era of 1890 to 1917, my father's time, drew many young people, including him, to minister and teach in foreign lands. Now the same motivation and personal commitment must send the message carriers to our own underclass. We will have to settle for limited success, but what success is possible may just save the nation.

The second group is comprised of a significant number of people who come from backgrounds where religion was likely as not to be a part of their family's life. Exposed to more ideas than similar people in past generations, confronted by old rules that did not seem to fit new conditions, they either rebelled against or wandered away from their religious traditions. But as most of us, they will eventually seek purpose, understanding of themselves, and a society that reflects their personal good tendencies toward justice, peace, freedom of speech and movement, and safety for themselves and others. They will not all buy into the same theological doctrine, nor will they all associate to the same degree with an organized church. For the most part, they are searchers. When they are ready, they will listen to reasonable explanation. What they will share is a summons to honesty, both personal and public. They will ask that people be accountable for their actions, including themselves. They can be aroused by a sense of justice. They can rekindle a work ethic, and even insist on it. They will listen to reasons why people must share with one another, and they will be persuaded to share. They will be ready to find and understand the spirit of God that is within them.

They have the background through family life and education to respond to a call for shared values. Integrity is not beyond their understanding. They have to define their beliefs more clearly so that they may be more firmly committed to them. The message they must understand is that a moral code of behavior imbedded deeply in the religious tradition of their society is the best guide for survival, for each personality, and for all together. That practical insight will be the core of the revival. Specific moral acts and requirements will follow from it. To be moral makes sense. It may be difficult to achieve, but simple to understand. Morality is a long-range survival kit, and people should require it in all segments of their society. It is accomplished through a core of shared values that determine acceptable behavior and laws that define and enforce that behavior.

Will the church be a generating force in the renewal of America? It has been in the past, but as I inferred previously, more people are farther removed from it today. Will they listen? Is the church ready for the challenge?

The fundamentalist churches accepted the challenge. At best they have increased their adherents, given millions of people a simple, straightforward set of beliefs to guide them, and set forth standards for public morality. At worst, some of their most prominent leaders with their sim-plistic gospel have succumbed to the complexities of greed and the lust for power. The problem for the fundamentalists is that their perception and requirements cannot possibly attract consideration from millions of peo-ple who must actively engage in the quest for a high public morality. There may be many yet uncalled to whom their message may one day sound loud, clear, and captivating, but there are more who will never hear their trum-pet no matter how loudly and seductively played. Can religion then be diversified enough and strong enough to call a diverse population to the standards of public morality America needs to survive?

Who will appeal to the majority of people, most of them in the sec-ond group that I described? Can there be revival without the church, a revival that will speak to the spirits of our citizens? I don't think so. It is the responsibility of the church. The fundamentalists are a power, but their generator has its limits. I see the churches of "main line" Protes-tantism and the congregations that have been spawned by that tradition as the source of an enlightened call to personal and public morality. I see them as being able to adjust their vocabulary and open their thinking to reach the many minds of America. I see the possibility of the church attracting good minds, the kind that do the thinking which finally refines itself into popular belief. My hope may be a "long shot," but I know that no past American revival has transpired without the Protestant church itself being the center of renewal. The message must be one of sharing rather than destruction through greed, of the judicious use of authority rather than the dominance of power, or the satisfaction in honest work instead of the morally crippling condition brought on by sloth, the joy and fulfillment of faith rather than the hopelessness of cynicism, and love of neighbor and family rather than the anger reflected in violence. This is an old gospel, as old as the church itself, and it needs to be effectively told to each generation just as it was so effectively told at the beginning by Jesus of Nazareth. It's the only way to go. We need to see it bear fruit in our national life.

The Church and the Liberal
Arts and Sciences: An Opinion

FALL 2000

T HE CHURCH IS OFTEN IN TENSION BETWEEN ITS ROLE AS THE guardian of eternal truth and its exploration in fields of knowledge that provide for new insight. The monks in medieval monasteries discovered ancient manuscripts bringing Plato, Aristotle, and other Greek thinkers into intellectual play in the development of Western thought in ways that ultimately changed Christian theological understanding, and the way the Christian religion was practiced. Copernicus, Galileo, and others involved in scientific investigation made discoveries accepted today, yet in their time did not match the belief held by the church. These were Christian scholars who unsettled the theology of their day yet remained in their religious tradition. Their ideas eventually prevailed throughout the western Christian world as the church adjusted to and learned from the discovered knowledge without surrendering its core message of forgiveness and redemption.

In the development of the United States, learning and worship are closely related—even intertwined. The western church, both Protestant and Catholic, came with the European settlers. By the nineteenth century, the building of a school followed soon after the church sanctuary, and schools played a role in communal life dating to the seventeenth and eighteenth centuries. Colleges began in the colonial period because parishioners wanted an educated clergy. Higher education in America moved across the country with the frontier, sponsored by the churches of the pioneers and immigrants. The curriculum in these colleges was comprised of the liberal arts and sciences. Over the years the courses that comprised a liberal arts curriculum changed and expanded, but to be educated meant to know the fields that encompassed human experience from the beginning to the present.

If the church knew, preached, and taught God's eternal truth, why were many of its members so committed to learning? Of course, some of the curriculum was intended mostly to study what was necessary to know more fully the approved theology. But science and philosophy could always lead to uncharted places, and history and literature open the mind to the way others lived and thought. There is within human consciousness, perhaps even the subconscious, the desire to know and feel sure about the truth, and also to use the mind and spirit to continually make the unknown known. The human desire for certainty and the desire to acquire knowledge that has the potential to undermine that certainty is a paradox in the human experience. The twentieth-century theologian, Reinhold Niebuhr, claimed that we may well come closest to the truth in paradoxical situations. The church lives in the paradox of proclaiming truth and discovering truth. The discovering part is found in the church's sponsorship of education throughout its development in the west from the cathedral schools and early European universities to the rich liberal arts tradition that permeates higher education in America.

The learning moves in two directions: first, it leads to objective, new knowledge for all who care to contemplate it; second, it adds to an individual's capacity for deeper personal understanding, for the understanding of relationships between and among people, and for a relationship to nature. Each person who delves seriously into history, philosophy, literature, mathematics, chemistry, biology, art, music, and the social sciences will not only increase his or her knowledge, but through that knowledge, deepen the spirit as well. This second kind of learning often enhanced by the first is personal. Each person who embarks upon it must have the will to do it.

A person can encourage, assist, and enable another to learn; but the learning is individual. It makes one more sensitive and brings with it a fullness of spirit.

In the New Testament, Jesus tells Nicodemus that one must have a second birth, a rebirth of the spirit. In the historical teaching of the Christian church that rebirth comes with the embrace of Jesus as the Son of God and Savior from sin and death. The original intent of the western church in its embrace of learning may have been to seek greater understanding of this mystery expressed in Jesus' words to Nicodemus. The church functions then as a proclaimer and a seeker of truth as it leads individuals to a rebirth of the spirit. Knowledge properly sought, learned, and applied contributes to the transformation of people and, thus, to their spiritual growth.

Though education and religion were essential functions of the church throughout most of western civilization, education today is sponsored, supported, and to a degree controlled by secular society more than it is by the church. Yet wherever the human mind roams in its search for knowledge and understanding it is dealing with the stuff that shapes future beliefs and interpretations, including those held within the church. The church is likely to continue indefinitely because it has demonstrated a capacity for reform. Whenever humans try to take charge of God and create God in their image, knowledge about life and nature undermines them. Open again to revelation through knowledge as well as need, a new church emerges. The process isn't neat. It does not necessarily bring unity. It takes a long time.

Periodically, the human race has to peel away the anxiety that is covered up by misplaced certainty in some cases and cynicism in others. In the people where that process is completed, forgiveness and redemption live, and where those people join together, the church lives as it should. The proclaiming and seeking, the knowing and the seeking to know, are where we live if we want to live best. We in the church can proclaim the truth and at the same time be open to new understanding of the truth we proclaim. There is God-given truth, but we are not the authors of that truth. We seek it. Perhaps that is why over the centuries the wisest thinkers in the church advocated a liberal education. They knew that human beings needed to use all that was available to them in the seeking. To calibrate correctly the tension between proclaiming and seeking, knowing and not knowing, certainty and uncertainty, confidence and humility is the task for the true church. Preaching the gospel and advocating liberal arts education is an important way towards meeting that task.

Speech to the
Campus Community

COOK-DEWITT CENTER
APRIL 17, 2001

I HAVE NOT COUNTED THE NUMBER OF TIMES I HAVE ADDRESSED THE college and now the university community since I arrived on January 15, 1969. There was a first time that I don't remember. This is the last and I will remember. On the Sunday after announcing that I would retire on June 30, 2001, worshipping in church, I was feeling sentimental, and to close the service we sang an equally sentimental hymn. It is a highly dramatic hymn; one might think schmaltz well describes it. My mood at the time contributed to personalizing one of the verses, relating it to our University and the meaning of a long career. The hymn is entitled, "Hail the Glorious Golden City," and here is the verse: "Hail the Glorious Golden City / and the work that we have builded, / oft with bleeding hands and tears, / oft in error, oft in anguish, / will not perish with our years; / it will live and shine transfigured, / in the final reign of right; / it will pass into the splendors / of the City of the Light."

A dash of nineteenth-century optimism finds a home within my heart. I substitute Grand Valley for Glorious Golden City at the beginning and for City of the Light at the end. In that edited verse you have my idealized version of what we, together, have been doing and our hopes for our efforts. This is not my time to lay before you an agenda. You have tabled most of my recent recommendations anyway. This is my time to thank you for being special colleagues in a special enterprise. As I do so, I will share with you the characteristics of a successful university building—a city of the light. There are four of them: ownership, authority, commitment, and sense of mission.

After my speech at the Grand Forum, an attorney friend asked me who owned Grand Valley. I gave a traditional answer about the trustees controlling the corporation and the corporation's relationship to the state. He didn't challenge me then, but he wrote me a letter describing a turning point in the history of western civilization when legal ownership was redefined.

Before then, ownership was not defined so narrowly in terms of personal property. In the Middle Ages, land was the basis of wealth. In those days the concept of outright ownership of land was foreign to legal thinking. No one owned land in the modern sense of the term—except God. Rather, one held an interest of one kind or another in a particular piece of land either permanently or for a determinable period of time. My friend, in posing the question, was suggesting that a university is owned more in the medieval sense than the post-sixteenth-century legal view of ownership that presently defines property and institutional disputes. Universities must be owned by several constituencies if they are to succeed, and the owners must be conscious of that ownership. A state university needs citizens to claim ownership. There is no doubt that football and basketball teams, comprised of pseudo-students who are in college only to play ball, bring attention to their universities and create a sense of ownership on the part of citizen fans—many of whom walk around with baseball caps worn backwards and with insignias touting their favorite team. We have not chosen that route, nor would it likely be open to us. For us, we attempt to lay hold of citizen interest and loyalty by demonstrating what we can do to enhance and even sustain their quality of life.

Citizen ownership manifests itself for a state university through elected officials. Those who work at the institution, including students, should have intense interest in those citizen representatives. The representatives must know that the university, its programs and people, are important to those whom they represent. They become owners for the people. A synergy for progress evolves when the representatives of the people work professionally to assist the university, and the faculty and staff at the university work professionally to further the objectives of the society.

Our university is particularly fortunate because so many citizens in our region appreciate what Grand Valley can do to enhance the quality of life around us. They have been persuaded to help us achieve goals, goals that we share, and goals that were unachievable without their resources and active good will. They have bought into our mission. They are owners.

In the future, it is in the university's interest to extend the circle of owners. We will always be the region's university. We will always be a Michigan state university, and we should find more throughout the state who take ownership. We can be a national university. Without neglecting our home and state base, I think the national challenge will make for interesting careers in Grand Valley's future.

The faculty and staff should feel that they belong, and in their belonging, have an ownership stake. In academia there is often a tension between loyalty to a field and loyalty to the institution. Loyalty to a field untempered by loyalty to the institution is likely to lead to more divisions, less interest in students, and acrimony. A university whose ethos encourages a feeling of ownership for the institution itself is likely to have professors and staff with long careers devoted to it, giving it the stability and personal investment that accompanies long careers. Of course, important contributions are made by those who, for the right reasons, move from the university. But it is best if the history of a university reveals tenure of many years by many people of high quality and good will, by people whose commitment of time shows that they feel they own a piece of the place.

The students who come as traditional eighteen-year-old freshmen come to the university filled with expectations accompanied by some fear. Those who engage and succeed are candidates for ownership. That engagement is fostered by good teaching and stimulating campus life. The university's challenge is to encourage the student to make the ownership life long—for the alumni will do as much to determine the future of the university as those who currently staff it. By intense loyalty or neglect they will make the difference. So it is crucial to devote thought, time, and resources to keeping alumni member owners of the place that launched them into adulthood.

Our university, as many modern academies of higher education, graduates many who, when enrolled, are labeled non-traditional students. They are often older, employed, married, and part-time. When they are students, they have obligations and distractions that discourage involvement leading to ownership, yet the benefits of education for them are as great as they are for the traditional students. Though more of a challenge for the university, they must be brought closer, and their strength and resources into play as the university moves towards its destiny.

Ownership, then, is not limited to who has legal title to the property or who can give or revoke the charter. Ownership belongs to all who participate in decisions at all levels, to all who devote time to the work of the university, and to those whose identity is connected in some way to the university. These are the participants, whether on campus or off. These are the owners.

The owners of an enterprise, through clearly defined lines of authority, through tradition, through strength of personality, through political process, through numerous paths to influence, or carried by the force of perceived public necessity, make the decisions for the University. Power is the omnipresent element that determines what is done and what is not done. It can flow in a democratic process or an authoritarian one. It can be tempered by inclusiveness or it can be ruthless in the way it is expressed. It can be thoughtless in its exercise or wise. It can lead to right decisions or wrong ones. When it coalesces, it is more likely to bring progress. When it is jealously guarded, it becomes more difficult to make progress. When people trust its exercise, the climate for right decisions improves. When there is lack of trust, there is likely to be stalemate. The acceptance of the power centers within the university, the acceptance of the appropriate use of power by individuals entitled to use it, the acceptance of the wisest judgments put forth in dealing with university issues, the respect for academic traditions when applied to the good of the whole rather than the protection of the destructive, and the consideration and inclusion of alumni and friends in some decisions will lead to the university becoming the best it can be.

The constitutional responsibility within Michigan state universities is easily understood. The power of the people flows to the Governor who appoints Board members who are entrusted with that power. They are affirmed by the State Senate. When duly confirmed, they together appoint a President, responsible to them, to be the chief executive officer and visionary. She or he is ultimately responsible for the appointment of other officers and deans—though by academic tradition, that power is shared by groups affected by those appointments. Faculty governance, administrative committees, and student senates all exercise power. In some areas each group makes definitive judgments; in others their decisions influence the final decision. Consensus is sought and the attempt to reach it should be a priority for all. Though disagreement and confrontation over disagreement is inevitable, it is ardently to be avoided.

There are many reasons for our university's success, for our ability to meet in a timely fashion the objectives our mission requires of us. The way that power is exercised and flows throughout the institution is different from most among Michigan's state universities. From my point of view, the wisest decision made by a majority of faculty on several occasions was to reject collective bargaining with its built-in adversarial approach. For years I have watched our sister institutions attempt to reach decisions through the collective-bargaining process. I have yet to see major benefits and, at some of the universities, the process, with its accompanying attitudes, has arrested their development. To resort to it because of a perceived or real grievance places unexpected limits on a university that will indefinitely undermine possibilities for excellence. There are other ways that groups within a university can address poor management and arbitrary, capricious decision-making. I have observed them, and the aggrieved group as well as the institution and, ultimately, the students have been well served. I wish I had more time today to analyze this issue in depth, but that will have to wait for a memoir.

I realize that some are committed to the collective-bargaining model for higher education, and I do not judge their competency as professors by that commitment. Many academics, however, prefer to stay away from organized faculties. With the market becoming what it is, they will locate jobs where they find the compatibility they seek. I think Grand Valley's interest is in being as attractive as possible to them. The same holds for administrators, especially presidents.

Stefan Zweig writes in *The Right to Heresy*, "Every nation, every epoch, every thoughtful human being, has again and again to establish the landmarks between freedom and authority: for in the absence of authority, liberty degenerates into license, and chaos ensues; and authority becomes tyranny unless it is tempered by freedom." Here are set forth the principles for an operational model of a university: authority so the institution responds as it should and moves forward, and freedom so people can be fulfilled and empowered in their own lives. The grease that makes this model operate smoothly is wisdom.

We move to a third characteristic. Some of the characteristics I am discussing overlap. Commitment is similar to ownership and comes by conscious decision. Power exists and has the potential for inducing irrational behavior. In talking about commitment I begin with the conditions necessary for it. Each job at the university is important to some aspects of its operation; therefore, it deserves the respect of all jobholders. Some have heavier demands, all require their own talents, but no position is intrinsically better than another. Arrogance because one is better than another is unsustainable. Of course, there are functions that are closer to the heart of the university's mission than others, but the failure of anyone in his or her job affects, in a large or small way, how the university operates just as success enhances it. With every job ascribed its dignity, there can be a common understanding about employment leading to the possibility of commitment.

The common understanding is not enough. People work for people and with people. The interpersonal relationships are the climate of employment. If the climate is pleasant, people enjoy and like the university, and usually stay. If it is unpleasant, "they're outta here" as soon as they find another place. Attention to best practices in supervision and to appropriate behavior amongst colleagues is high on my list of university priorities. When we seek people to fill positions, we appropriately concern ourselves with their professional qualifications. I wish we could find their neurosis quotient as well.

Fairness is an ideal, an ideal that is elusive as we try to put it in practice. Though we are likely to agree on a definition of the concept, our disagreements come when it is applied to specific individuals and situations. Yet if a person is to feel a commitment to the university, he or she must feel that fairness is a concern, and attempts are made to have more rather than less of it. With this understanding, even a few personal negative feelings can be overcome on the path to commitment. Problems of salaries, benefits, and promotions are the nerve endings embodied in this concept. The domestic partner benefits issue, the most recent of the controversial ones, will test the loyalty and interest of owners as it works its way to resolution. We will see whether or not past commitment can be sustained, or whether domestic partner benefits is a single issue that determines one's commitment or lack of it.

To take the leap of commitment, a person needs the resources to do the job in a manner that meets professional objectives. Frustration in this matter usually leads to an early exit, and university administrators and colleagues should have their own antennae well placed to pick up the frustration. There are times when the expectations are beyond the university's capacity to meet them. There are times when they can be met. Default is unnecessary.

So if the conditions are there, the possibility of faculty and staff commitment to staying and feeling loyal will turn into a reality. The university, comprised of its owners in the medieval sense, benefits from the force of the commitment to it. Professors and staff "walk an extra mile" for the students. Students, at a formative stage in their lives, respond with appreciation and effort to succeed. Faculty take pride in the students' response. The quality of work improves. All take pride in that. The campus is beautiful and well maintained. The pleasure of attractive surroundings begins to effect positive feelings and behavior. In good times and bad the management of resources is diligent, efficient, and effective. Good people, both students and employees, are attracted to join the community because they find at the university people who work hard and believe in their university. Others hear positive comments by the believers, and the university's successes become contagious. Am I a reincarnation of Pollyanna? I don't think so. I have not dwelt on the dark side, nor have I analyzed our failure to achieve commitment. And they exist. I have described, however, what the commitment by so many of you has brought to our university in the past decade.

The first generation of Grand Valley faculty and staff are leaving the stage. We are all gone or going soon. We have given this place, I believe, a larger dose of commitment than most new state universities. That dose has helped make some special things happen here, and my hope is that you who carry this place forward keep the commitment quotient high. You need to do that to see that Grand Valley earns the place in higher education that is waiting for it.

When I arrived here thirty-two years ago last January, I found a faculty devoted to the liberal arts and a college with a core curriculum that reflected that devotion. As I leave, the university, now complex, now home for professional programs defined by their excellence, I leave with the liberal arts core changed, but excellent and intact. During this long course there have been disagreements about the direction of the institution; there have been changes in that direction. Through it all, I have held to the belief formed in high school, in college, and at home that the open door to being an educated person is through the liberal arts curriculum. Holding to that principle is the foundation on which Grand Valley will build itself into a premier institution. And what is the mission of this premier institution? The sense of mission is the final characteristic of a university that I will discuss and commend to you. You must know where you are going and how you propose to get there. Over the years, I have attempted to describe Grand Valley's mission. To me the definition was clear, but I don't think I adequately made my thoughts articulate or, if I did for some, persuaded others to endorse it. On this, my last address to you as President, I need to say once again where I was trying to lead. This is my coda, my repetition of a theme.

First, Grand Valley can be the best among the state universities who teach undergraduates. This should be the unchallenged first priority for the university.

Second, the university should encourage the research of faculty who want or, for accreditation reasons, must undertake it. Areas for special research commitment must be identified and aided to a high level of competency. For instance, I believe the Annis Water Resources Institute can become a fresh water research leader in the nation. The opportunities to collaborate with the Van Andel Institute will evolve and be intriguing.

Third, Grand Valley should be an international comfort zone. The curriculum should be infused with international material and experience. People from around the world should move easily to and from our campuses, and our Michigan students should move as easily into the world, gaining experience and language skills.

Fourth, as Grand Valley establishes itself as a cosmopolitan university, known throughout the country for effective teaching, commitment to west Michigan and the special needs of the region should remain a priority.

The dangers that confront a university in relation to its mission are twofold. First there is inertia, and second there is a fall back to graduate-school-learned principles about higher education that hinder the development of a university in a new time in a special place. The best way to cope with these omnipresent dangers is for a sense of mission to pervade the campus. Effort and energy is directed to serving those whom the mission calls the university to serve. For Grand Valley this is particularly urgent because we are in the state of becoming. We are not yet what we are going to be. That is not true of most of our sister institutions. I suggest that Saginaw Valley and possibly Oakland are similar. Of course, any institution can choose not to fulfill its highest destiny. Arrested development is a fact we see and understand.

For Grand Valley there is a need to reorganize in the health area if the university is to reach its full potential. Other academic and administrative areas are worth examination too. Are they all organized for progress? This is threatening activity for it may lead to changes, but if the need for change is the way to improvement, do you have the courage to make it?

I see so clearly that an Associate Degree in Holland is the best way to fulfill an aspect of Grand Valley's mission. I understand that it may have no professional effect for a person who opposes it. Yet, in the long and short run, it has educational and social ramifications. More than that, failure to move forward will bring political and economic consequences.

Inertia and views that are not influenced by Grand Valley's intense sense of mission dribble away opportunities and even responsibilities. I have mentioned two that now sit on your table. I would take them off as soon as possible. That may be reason enough for some in the room to think, "Be gone and be gone quickly."

As my Presidential days near their end, a work by C. S. Lewis comes to mind. Lewis, an eminent medieval and Renaissance literature scholar, better known for his second career as a writer of Christian literature, wrote a book entitled *Surprised by Joy*. He states that, "It is not settled happiness but momentary joy that glorifies the past." Settled happiness ranks high with me in my personal life, but as I reflect on my career it is those moments of joy that come when a goal is achieved or an obstacle overcome that gave me the satisfaction, energy, and emotional reinforcement to move on to the next objectives with faith and positive thought. Though one hopes to reach objectives and circumvent obstacles, when success comes there is an element of surprise that accompanies the joy. I don't know why. I do know that gratitude is the feeling that overwhelms both Nancy and me now, and we ask the question that has an imperative quality as well as interrogative: "Why have we been chosen for this task, for so many years, to influence the establishment of standards and traditions of a fine university?" If we have made a contribution, it has come back to us in fulfillment, satisfaction, important relationships, and fun—all in abundance. We understand the meaning of being blessed.

I have heard that some apprehension inserts itself in conversations when there is talk about the three of us to whom you have been long accustomed leave during a period of three months. You can be encouraged that Tim Schad, Ron VanSteeland's replacement, is taking to his job with the skill and enthusiasm that would make even Ron proud. There is no better guard at Glenn Niemeyer's gate than John Gracki whom you know well and who knows you as well. The search for a new Provost will be inclusive and far-reaching. With John in place there is no need to rush. As for the person selected to be Grand Valley's third president, he, in my estimation, is the right choice. Mark Murray is a thoughtful person and he is generous in spirit. He is experienced in the ways of leadership and operations. He knows politics and he knows the territories where Grand Valley must make its mark. I will surrender my seal of office to him confident that he will accept it with the determination, intelligence, and goodwill to be successful as President. I believe he will commit to Grand Valley as I have committed. I believe he will carry a strong sense of mission to his work, as I have to mine. I believe working here with you he will come to love the university as I love it. After a short time the bright light of a new administration will focus attention on its agenda and yours, and memories of the former players will glimmer dimly and take their assigned place in the past.

Emerson wrote, "A friend is a person with whom I may be sincere. Before him or her I may think aloud." For many minutes you have allowed me to think aloud. You are my friends, or so I consider you. On many occasions you and others have indulged me as I thought aloud amongst you. We have come today to the last time I will do so as President of the University. I have been asked about my future association with you, and there will be one. When I am asked I think about the early days when we traveled to the University of Sarajevo to establish an exchange relationship. Over several trips we were entertained often by university or government officials. On each of these occasions there would be in attendance an old, retired, partisan hero, noted for some significant act during the Second World War. He was a true warhorse. This hero, until his retirement, had usually held a professorship or a high government position. He was given deferential treatment, and usually gave a toast at the appropriate time. The food and drink were plentiful and always of good quality. I thought I might enjoy serving that function at Grand Valley events, and I may volunteer.

As I wind down, I turn to the poets for expression. From Byron, "Fare thee well and if forever, still forever fare thee well." From Milton, "Farewell happy fields where joy forever dwells." Well, that may be going a bit too far; joy doesn't forever dwell very many places. From Shakespeare, "Fare thee well; The elements be kind to thee and make thy spirits all of comfort." Again Shakespeare, "Sweets to the sweet: farewell." And gain "Farewell and standfast." Finally, to Byron again. I like English Romantic poets, and that is enough to send me on my way. I understand English Romantic poets are out, but on to Byron, "Farewell! A word that must be and have been—a sound which makes us linger;—yet farewell."

Upon his retirement from the Army after being recalled from Japan and Korea, General Douglas MacArthur was invited to address the Congress of the United States. In closing he turned to military lore for a quote. He said, "Old soldiers never die, they just fade away." I think that is true for my profession as well. "Old Presidents never die, they just fade away."

In the Name of God

FOUNTAIN STREET CHURCH

JUNE 23, 2002

F IFTY YEARS AGO THIS SUMMER I HAD MY ROAD-TO-DAMASCUS EXPERI-
ence, except it was on the road to Sarajevo when, as a twenty-year-
old, I gave up guilt. I tell you about it because even this
life-assisting revelation hasn't secured me from occasional lapses. One of
those lapses brings me to the pulpit this morning. I usually summon the
courage to decline invitations to preach sermons. But after a few years of
saying no to those authorized to fill out the summer preaching slate at
Fountain Street, I felt guilty at not meeting a responsibility that the invitation implies I accept, and I accepted.

Not long after the event when I relieved myself of guilt's burden, I was
urged by several friends, with whom I had considerable personal and religious compatibility at the time, to become a preacher. This higher calling
never quite captured me because as I waited for it to awaken my desire and
consuming interest, an inner voice louder and more persistent said, "What
can you possibly say to people each week that will meet their expectations?" I was brought up in a period when two sermons a week were
expected, one in the morning and one at night. In our town founded by

Dutch immigrants, even a third Sunday sermon in Dutch was required by bilingual clergymen.

All this I say to you because I made my decision, and here I am not sticking to it. Your attendance here helps me assuage my guilt, but it does not make me a preacher. Yet, I must say something. The September 11 destruction in New York City was perpetrated by Islamic Fundamentalists who take issue with our way of life and acted in the name of Allah, in the name of God. Terror justified by religion has been on my mind so that is what I am going to talk about this morning.

In the twelfth century, a monk at the Abby of St. Albans in England wrote detailed accounts of how Turks murdered Christians and even in cannibalistic terms described how they devoured the tenderest parts. Whether fact or more likely fiction, it didn't matter. The stage was set for crusaders when Christians in God's name would march and sail to the east to route the infidel from Christianity's holy places. For centuries the Christian agenda was set, accompanied by land grabs, church-imperial politics, and the accumulations of wealth.

In the sixteenth century, Henry VIII separated the church in England from the Catholic Church and took upon himself and the crown the leadership of Christ's church in his realms. He confiscated church property, married, divorced and executed wives, beheaded his chancellor, Thomas More, who would not recognize his right to be God's vicar of all England. All this Henry did invoking God's name, for it was politically necessary for him to do so.

While on the other side of the channel, French Catholic rulers determined to wipe out heresy and later Protestantism, making the St. Bartholomew's Day massacre both a fact and symbol of their intent.

In the seventeenth century, the Lord Protector of England, Oliver Cromwell, cut a swath through Catholic Ireland with his army, which through the centuries has brought Ireland to the hopeless conflict between Protestants and Catholics in the North. Cromwell was a devout man. All of this began in the name of God.

From 711 when the Saracens were defeated in France and pushed south into the Iberian Peninsula until the sixteenth century when the Turks were turned away from the gates of Vienna, fear of conquest by

Moslems pervaded the Christian west. Now five centuries later a virulent strain of the Prophet Mohammad's religion has gained the world's attention, for in the name of Allah they are ready to kill those whom they call infidels. And leaders promise a paradise of untold pleasures to the youth they persuade to be their instruments of destruction to take out the enemy by destroying themselves.

Despite all the evidence that leads us to be disturbed about the consequences of religion, most of us came to our maturity expecting positive results for our lives from our religious experience. This leads to asking two questions. Where does religion come from, and why does it so often go wrong? The origin of the word *religion* yields some interesting definitions: to bind together is one; another, to be concerned; a third, to pay heed to. Out of the mists of the past these suggest human beings seeking commonalities, understandings that will help them survive together, paying heed to what they see and experience, and giving meaning to it—first in small numbers gathered together, then in tribes of people drawn together by geography and genetics. Later the evolution of human thought and communication made it possible for a leader of a people to embrace a religion and bring his people along with him. By then we can see that religion, a belief system, also had political and economic ramifications for those who embraced it. From the beginning it appears that the search for religion was the search by humans to save themselves from their worst instincts and invoke a power outside themselves for their protection. The search did not bring a uniformity of belief and practice, but it did have the common characteristic that all religions were perceived by their adherents as representing the truth.

In this long process of religious development from sophistication to sophistication, the need to pay heed to the power of God has not waned, but defining the power of God causes differences. In the Christian religion the essence and priorities are well defined in the gospels. Listen to some of Jesus' words: "You have learned that they were told love your neighbor, hate your enemy. But what I tell you is this: love your enemies and pray for your persecutors only so you can be children of your Heavenly Father who makes the sun arise on the good and bad alike. . . . If you love only those who love you, what reward can you expect? . . . There must be no limit to your goodness, as your Heavenly Father's goodness knows no bounds." The thought expressed by Jesus is revolutionary, advocating an approach to human life that was not found much, if at all, before his time, and as we have seen, not necessarily by those who proclaimed in his name afterwards.

Though I have not studied in depth world religions, the Christian faith, with the life of Christ and the compilation of the Bible, provided the human species insights and a way to new revelation. It is truly a way to save individuals from destroying themselves. Other religions have their way, and all seem to have common spiritualities.

If a good way is open to us, why do we so often pervert it in the name of God? First we must, I believe, look back to the origin of life. There accompanies the spark of life an instinctive need to protect it even at the loss of other lives. Certainly it is the way with animals, and in the end it fails. No individual physical life lasts indefinitely. Add human consciousness to that need and there is an opening to an array of possibilities. The most prominent is the native aggression used to protect and sustain life in the unconscious manifesting itself consciously in human behavior. Life innately lives for itself, it is egotistic. Seeking and gaining power over others in ruthless ways is one of its expressions. The accumulation of unjustly gained possession is another. The failure of individuals or groups to deal thoughtfully and fairly with others is a sure sign. Our forbearers, in the mist of pre-history, groping for ways to define and cope with this characteristic, began to formulate religions for that purpose. Unfortunately, what they and what we today understand from experience and grace as a civilizing control of aggression's destructive tendencies is not universally held. The militant Islamist is much on our minds for in the name of God he unleashes ungodly aggression.

Second comes from discomfort with the unknown. Religion, since it is the avenue to truth, is expected to find all of it, definitely and definitively, and set aside the uneasiness of not knowing. There is a wide spectrum from the absolutist to the relativist. On the absolutist end we will find those, not all, who can kill, condemn, and cast out in the name of God. When I think of the young Americans who chose to study in schools of militant Islam, I see young men who are relieved of the burden of further searching and uncertainty. I see young men given opportunity to vent their aggression using the will of God in a way far removed from my understanding of God's will. I believe they have traded their revulsion of that which is degrading in our society for an evil alternative with the society they have embraced.

The theological structures with their certainties provide explanation for the greatest fear of what is not known to us. And the need for surety about afterlife may contribute to building theological systems of thought and behavior that carry with them exclusive and absolute tenets about all things. Those absolutes carry with them the danger of protracted battles both hot and verbal fought for generations until descendants who may not be held by true religious fervor are carrying on the fight by acculturation yet in the name of God. A total absolutist about religion assumes God's power. God then is made in man's image.

Ungodly aggression and unqualified absolutism always, it seems, infiltrate religions and sometimes make them function in the interests they were born to combat. So if religion is "on the label" it does not guarantee what it purports to deliver. What then should we look for to find genuine religion? We should realize that religion, to have its desired effect in the life of the individual, is comprised of concepts to be experienced, not facts to believe. "The greatest of these is love," writes Paul to the Corinthians. Our Christian heritage, and probably that of all great religions, is rooted in the message of unconditional love. God is defined by love. Jesus is seen as God's gift of redeeming love, and love is a concept we can understand. We feel love for others, we feel it coming to us, we experience different aspects and intensities of it. We know our lives work better when it is present with us and around us. When we observe those who are deprived of it, we know their lives are less complete than ours. We can get our minds and feelings around the concept of love. So as difficult as it is to practice, we know what Jesus meant when he said, "Love your enemies."

Humility is the best check on the excesses brought about by aggression and absolutism. It's a check on the ego. For that reason, after love, it is my favorite concept. Humility enables holding beliefs, seeking and having insights without insisting that yours is the "last word." It sets aside arrogance and self-righteousness. Humility does not prevent you from defending yourself or your faith if threatened from without, but it keeps you from threatening others in the name of God.

Reverence is the capacity for deep respect, respect for living creatures, for the wonders of nature, for the power of this spirit in our lives, for good deeds that transform life from an anxiety-filled experience into one of caring and loving. Reverence begets gratitude, one of the best of all feelings because reverence is also a way of perceiving life. If reverence is part of your make-up, you are grateful for the beauty you see all around you. The other side of the reverence coin is the concern and even anger you feel when reverence for life is violated. Those who attack and kill in the name of religion may be devout, but they are not reverent.

Grace is a concept that helps us live in peace with ourselves, to accept what we don't know without giving up or striving to know more. In the greater scheme we fit, and we are all right. Grace is a word for the relationship of the spirit of God within us to the spirit of God beyond us. "Amazing Grace how sweet the sound to save a wretch like me." We all sing it, those nineteenth-century words, in one of America's favorite melodies. Most of us have had wretched experiences. Most of us have regretted actions, thoughts and feelings. They are not burdens to carry forever. There is a spirituality that envelopes us and connects with the spirit within when we allow it to happen. Feeling grace is more complex, I believe, than feeling love, but it can be felt. Love must be understood before grace abounds. When you understand grace, you understand your place, and the spirit within and without pretty well guide the flow of life given to you. A person in a state of grace, I don't think, can practice religion as a reaction to the evil perceived in others, killing people because they don't believe correctly, spewing hatred as the militant Islamists do today.

I am tempted to examine humor as a fifth religious concept, but I need more thought time on that one. If the Moslem clerics, the Irish Catholics and Protestants, the Jewish leaders and Palestinian leaders would laugh more, I'm sure they would advocate killing less.

Religious belief is spiritual blood carrying spiritual nutrients through-out our beings. If it is carried by supple arteries it replenishes our spirits and also our minds, keeping them open, receptive and growing. If the arteries harden that blood cannot get through and nourish love, humility, reverence, and grace, the essential qualities of true religion. True religion then dies, yet in its name horrible events take place.

A Great Leader
of Higher Education

Mark A. Murray

Mark A. Murray became the third president of Grand Valley State University in 2001, following a twenty-year career in state government and education. Murray held a variety of positions in state government including treasurer, budget director, director of the Department of Management and Budget, and acting director of the Family Independence Agency. As special policy advisor to the governor, Mr. Murray was responsible for a variety of initiatives aimed at K–12 public school reform. He served as a member of the Board of Education for the City of Detroit and vice president for finance and administration at Michigan State University.

T HE WORK OF LEADING AN ENTERPRISE CAN BE DECEPTIVELY SIMPLE. All it takes is a sound strategy that is well executed. This is a rule that has few exceptions. Of course, it is a great challenge to ensure that the strategy is sound and is open to occasional refinement. And the challenges of effective execution are unlimited.

Arend D. Lubbers was a great leader. During his tenure Grand Valley prospered. Not without trial. Not without occasional mistakes. But the State of Michigan, and particularly West Michigan, will be indebted to this man for many generations to come because of his passionate commitment to higher education, and because he developed sound strategies and executed them well while being responsive to the surprises and opportunities of a society in rapid change.

Don Lubbers's speeches will remain relevant for years to come because he addresses so well the core questions of higher education. His speeches are thoughtful and the topics are timely. Their enduring relevance and broad appeal are guaranteed because he touches the core issues of higher education that so obviously match many of the basic purposes of any human endeavor.

Don's speech on negativism reminds us of the cheap cynicism that pervades too much of higher education and too many of our most important endeavors. The cynicism of the day is fed by the many claims of simplistic truth, and the comfort of the armchairs in which so many critics sit. Our culture does so well ridiculing the bombasts and charlatans that it spills over to a general contempt for dedicated, principled leaders with their inevitable clay feet, and essential institutions with their inevitable flaws.

The speech on financial challenges reminds us of the current challenge of leading government-supported endeavors. We have a widespread consensus among the citizenry that government will provide a full range of services. There is an equally widespread consensus that the cost for such services is too high. In less than fifty years, a near universal expectation has arisen that government will provide health care for the uninsured, social support for unstable families, general public safety, widely available recreational opportunities, an expansive transportation infrastructure, the most modern national defense systems, improved public health, and high-quality education for all who seek it. There is nothing unwarranted in any of these hopes. However, there will not be the resources to accomplish all these lofty goals. And as it relates to higher education, the trend of many decades now is that students are asked to bear an ever-increasing share of the cost of their education. A public good becomes ever more a private good.

And most important, the speeches on education itself raise basic and intriguing issues. Why engage? What is the higher purpose of higher education? To use Martin Luther King's phrase, what is the "worthy objective" upon which we concentrate our minds and our hearts?

Universities engage in the search for new truths about nature—one of humankind's most noble and longstanding endeavors. We use and teach a method of investigation that is devoted to facts, reason, observation, a healthy skepticism, and precision of thought. These attributes show through in Don's observations as they did in his actions as leader.

Community building is a noble purpose in both the broader society and the university. Community is built through so many simple and complex steps of shared experience and effective communication. Our ability to understand what makes us the same and what makes us different offers an opportunity for better community. The university expands our ability to reach across time and culture to engage each other.

Improved material well-being is another worthy objective. Our universities provide skills and insights that allow individuals to help advance our collective productivity and to provide the innovations that have so dramatically improved material well-being in past decades. But universities can move us beyond material well-being to social well-being. Universities are a central intersection of economic innovation and cultural development.

It is no coincidence that there is such a strong historic link between commercial centers and cultural centers. Rome, Venice, Istanbul, Amsterdam, London, New York, and Shanghai are but a few examples. The drive of enterprise that forces individuals to cross culture, geography, and interest also enlivens more general intellectual and cultural inquiry. One of President Lubbers's great legacies will be the balanced blend of liberal and professional education that is the heart of Grand Valley, integrating the economic and cultural objectives of a public university.

President Lubbers focused on the spiritual moreso than many of his peers at public universities. Thankfully this concern with the spiritual has never been abandoned at Grand Valley. A deep restlessness exists within so many young people, and questions of purpose and meaning in life are close to the surface during these years in school. Purpose and meaning are found by many in the long-standing systems of religious belief, and President Lubbers spent considerable effort to elaborate on how a public university could serve as a leaven for personal spiritual development.

The life of this university is just beginning. A hundred years from now it will be known even more widely as a place of higher learning. A hundred years from now West Michigan will be even more obviously enriched by its graduates. Just as this nation still builds on the century-old insights and leadership of Theodore Roosevelt, Grand Rapids still builds on the economic leadership of Sligh, Widdicomb, and other late nineteenth-century furniture entrepreneurs. So, too, Grand Valley in the opening years of the twenty-second century will look back at President Don Lubbers as a figure of essential importance in the history of this institution and great importance for all of public higher education in the second half of the twentieth century. Indeed, Arend D. Lubbers has offered inspiration and sound advice that will have enduring meaning for higher education and the broader community.